bOOk Of SHAdOWS tAROt

As Above, So Below

Barbara Moore
Artwork by Gregorz Krisinsky, Simone Gabrielli, Franco Rivolli, Pietro Scola di Mambro, Sabrina Ariganello, Alessia Pastorello.

© Lo Scarabeo 2012

Lo Scarabeo
Via Cigna 110, 10155 - Torino, Italy
Tel: 011 283793 - Fax: 011 280756
E-mail: info@loscarabeo.com
Internet: http://www.loscarabeo.com

Printed by: Shanghai Offset

First Edition: May 2012
First Reprint: January 2013

BOOK OF SHADOWS
TAROT

INDEX

INTRODUCTION

Introduction

A Book of Shadows is a very personal journal kept by many witches, Wiccans, and pagans as a record of their spiritual journey, ritual practices, and magical workings. The pages reflect the personality of their creator and may be filled with recipes, references, personal notes, and sketches. Pictures may be glued to some pages. Charts of correspondences may be scattered throughout. While there my be a chronological feel to the Book, many pages will have jottings and notes added later, perhaps months or years after a particular reading, ritual, or spell took place. In this way, the practitioner has a complete record of the experience from beginning to conclusion. Adjustments can be made, lessons and insights reflected upon, and plans for the future formulated.

While a Book of Shadows often has a non-linear flavor, the tarot is often called an unbound book – a collection of pages that you can shuffle and lay out in any order. In addition to being an unbound book, tarot also has a history of being holder of knowledge. Our earliest records of the tarot come from the Renaissance and tell of a deck of cards used for playing games. However, the images on the trumps (what we now call the Major Arcana) reflected social mores and important teachings. Over time, the images evolved but are still often said to hold esoteric or spiritual teachings. The currently popular Rider-Waite-Smith (RWS) deck is said to contain teachings of the Golden Dawn. However, since apparently the designer, Arthur E. Waite, was sworn to secrecy, the deck conceals and confuses almost as much as it reveals.

In its own way, the tarot is a kind of Book of Shadows – except with images rather than words – an unbound, magical book filled with wisdom, guidance, and lessons. The tarot is like a Book of Shadows in another way, too. Just as the two companion decks in this set illustrate the twin reflections of Universal Energies and Personal Energies, the Major and the Minor Arcanas of a tarot deck also represent larger life events and everyday experiences. The Major

Arcana shows us the archetypal energies that show up in our lives in the form of life-changing situations, milestone events, or events beyond our control. The Minor Arcana is concerned with the ordinary events, the ups and downs, the fill our daily lives.

The *Book of Shadows Tarot* is a unique kit. It includes the tarot deck titled *As Above* and this book. In addition, the packaging includes a spot to store the companion deck, titled *So Below*. The titles are based on the Hermetic Principal of Correspondences (discussed with the Magician card). The idea is that what happens in the heavens or on a spiritual level is reflected on the physical plane. So the deck *As Above* reflects the teachings and beliefs of paganism, and *So Below* shows how magic and elemental energies affect our everyday lives. The decks are not only thematically connected but can also work together to do very special readings, as you will see in the last section.

The first deck, *As Above*, is a tarot deck designed to hold and express modern Pagan spiritual teachings. Pagan beliefs are broad and hardly unified, but we will discuss that momentarily. The Major Arcana cards represent some of the basic tenets while the Minor Arcana thoroughly explores elemental energies while providing foundations for further studies in the areas of astrology, the faces of the Goddess, the magic of the physical realm, and various forms of divination. Because each card is a portal into vast realms of knowledge and experience and because space in this book is limited, each section includes a reading list of excellent texts for further studies.

The second deck, *So Below*, is the companion to *As Above*, designed to compliment that deck and complete the analogy. While *As Above* focuses on the teachings and Universal Energies present in the world, *So Below* explores how we live those teachings in everyday life as well as how we experience and work with the Elements. *As Above* shows what exists and its nature. *So Below* shows how we experience all that exists.

You can think of the two decks as forming an hourglass shape, with *As Above*, of course, shaping top cup of the device and *So Below* forming the bottom. Here is where it gets interesting: the two Major Arcanas together form the funnel, that small point in an hourglass that divides the top from the bottom. For it is as we experience or embody the archetypes of our beliefs that we act as a channel bringing the Divine into this world. These two Arcana really do reflect each other quite nicely. In Chapter 2, you can find a section that explores their relationship.

The following section will present the cards in this deck. For those familiar with tarot and the RWS tradition, the Major Arcana will feel familiar, although they are not exact replications. Instead, the tenets of Paganism matched with each card resonate with the traditional meaning even if the image may look different from what you are used to. The Minor Arcana will look very different. No attempt was made to repeat the Golden Dawn teachings, the descriptions of Arthur E. Waite, or the compositions of Pamela Coleman Smith. Instead, each suit is completely redesigned to reflect specific teachings. These teachings still, of course, represent important energies in our lives and can be used for divination like any other tarot deck.

The next section explores the cards of the companion deck, *So Below*. In addition, this is where you will find an study of the unique relationship between the Major Arcana cards from both decks. Once you are familiar with the cards, you'll want to use them. The section on Spreads will get you started reading.

Before we delve into the cards, we need to lay a little groundwork.

Modern paganism is constantly evolving. Because it grows and changes, this spiritual path always feels fresh and organic; it absorbs and adapts new knowledge, understanding, and experience. This makes it, in many ways, a very practical religion. However, it does make it difficult to write about in general terms, as there are few ideas that are commonly agreed upon. Do understand that there will be points in this book with which some practicing pagans may not agree. It is the nature of neo-paganism to hold different opinions, discuss, and even disagree. In all things, including the reading of this book, consider the opinions and ideas of others, but in the end, as a friend of mine says, hold your own truth close and let others have theirs.

Neo-pagan religions are spiritual practices that are earth-based or that incorporate nature-centric philosophies, such a Wicca, Neo-Shamanism, or Neo-Druidism. Modern pagan practices are inspired by ideas about centuries-old Western European pagan rites and rituals. There is no governing body, although various groups and covens form around different traditions. There is no book or bible, no codified collection of rules or beliefs (in fact, most practitioners have their own personal holy book – their Book of Shadows). Instead, modern paganism is an experiential path and all practitioners are their own priestesses or priests. Because of the emphasis on direct contact with the gods, goddesses, and the Divine, this is a path of knowledge rather than faith. A pagan does not "believe" in, say, Brigid because she "knows" Brigid via a personal relationship with her.

Because of the basis in experience and the lack of dogma, paganism offers much freedom. With that freedom comes personal responsi-

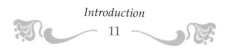

bility, which is further highlighted by one of paganism's most significant tenets: the immanence of the Divine. This means that the Divine is in all things (trees, rocks, animals, people, etc.), that all things are divine, and that everything is connected. This does not mean that things have consciousness, but that all things are sacred and should be treated as such. Determining how any particular thing and its immanent Divinity should be treated is part of each practitioner's personal responsibility.

While most pagans share the common beliefs of immanent Divinity, personal experience and responsibility, and a focus on nature, not all claim to practice magic. Magic is often described as the use of the energies of the Universe to manifest one's will on earth. This definition assumes a conscious understanding and manipulation of energy, sometimes called "will" or "intent." In fact, some say that intent is the most important element in magic. That may be true, but a deeper understanding of energy makes for more efficient and effective magic. Everything that exists is made of energy. Energy follows certain principles or laws – the seven Hermetic principles (again, see The Magician card). All of life follows these principles. It is the understanding and conscious use of these principles that constitutes magic.

The manipulation of energy to manifest desires in itself carries no judgment. However, this is about pagan magic, so our inherent nature-centric focus shapes our magical practice and application. Because we believe that all things are sacred and not in existence merely for our exploitation, we consider ourselves partnering with nature rather than controlling it. Because we believe all things are connected and divine, we seek to create magic for the greatest good for others, the earth, the Divine, and ourselves. Because we are on a spiritual path, we desire transformation and spiritual growth, and this is an important focus in our magic. That is not to say that we do not do magic for physical and/or personal needs. We often do. Part of paganism is a celebration of and a reverence for enjoyment of the physical world. A concise way to think about pagan magic is the intentional use of personal will to partner with nature to create change in the world for the greatest good of all.

> *A concise way to think about pagan magic is the intentional use of personal will to partner with nature to create change in the world for the greatest good of all.*

Freedom is a great benefit of a pagan worldview, but the lack of concrete, black and white rules governing good and bad or right and wrong mean that with freedom comes much responsibility. When discussing responsibility, magical practice, spiritual paths, it's natural to think about ethics. The principles of energetic behavior have no intrinsic judgment, rather like the Law of Gravity has no judgment. As pagans, we impose our own judgments and our own ethics. We know that just because one can do something doesn't mean that one should do something.

There are various reasons and caveats for being careful with magic. Two of the most popular are The Rule of Three and the Wiccan Rede. The Rule of Three is a philosophy that says whatever you do, good or bad, will come back to you three times. Most spiritual paths and folk wisdom include this type of exhortation. The Wiccan Rede is a prescription for behavior that exists in several forms. A common variation is "and it harm none, do what ye will," meaning that you can do anything you desire as long as it doesn't hurt anyone else.

These moral codes are fine. However, there is a more basic reason for behaving ethically and practicing magic responsibly. Because the Divine is immanent, all people (including ourselves) and all things are sacred and, as pagans, we wish treat them as such. We don't avoid harming others out of fear of retribution or a cosmic payback. We work from love and respect because that is how we approach the Divine. When deciding on responsible magic, we are encouraged to think things through carefully and look at the possible consequences of our actions. However, as humans, our perspective is limited, our knowledge of the facts often incomplete, and our thoughts not always objective. We may not really know what the consequences of something will be. Therefore, when working magic, many pagans end their spells with a statement that allows the wisdom of the Divine to override the spell. For example, "either this or something better, harming none" or "for the greatest good."

Pagan magic is more than following recipes to get results. It is an expression of a spiritual path requiring reflection and thought as well as knowledge and experience. A logical understanding of energy creates a strong foundation for effective magical work. Remember, though, that paganism is a very experiential path. There is no substitute for experiencing energy. Everything has its own unique blend of energy. By paying attention, you will find that you can see, sense, and feel energy. You will notice that anyone or anything's energy has various states. It can be functioning in a neutral state, it can be receptive, or it can be emotive. Because magic is about partnering with nature (energy), the better you understand it, the more likely you are to gain its cooperation and to work with it effectively.

This short introduction is just that – an opportunity to let you know a little bit about what is ahead and to share some important information that is not covered in the cards. There really wasn't much additional material to share because, as you will see, the cards provide an excellent format for spiritual teaching.

AS ABOVE

The Major Arcana

Early on in the tarot's history, the Major Arcana cards were not numbered. However, we are now quite accustomed to putting numbers on these cards. This provides a number of benefits. For example, many readers like to incorporate numerology into their readings. Others consider the numerical sequence as a variation on the Hero's Journey (a concept popularized by Joseph Campbell and, in tarot circles, is called the Fool's Journey). As for me, I think one of the most practical aspects is so that beginners can easily find the card they are looking up as they first learn tarot. Mundane, perhaps, but from a beginner's standpoint, it is very much appreciated.

Following this useful tradition, the Major Arcana cards in this deck are indeed numbered. And their divinatory meanings are repeated in a list at the end of this chapter in numerical order, for easy reference. However, the bulk of this chapter explores the Major Arcana cards in groups that do not relate to the numbers printed on them. Instead, they are divided into different classifications that illustrate various aspects of Pagan beliefs.

The Major Arcana cards in this deck follow the archetypal ideas expressed in traditional tarot decks but express them from a pagan point of view. In this way, the deck becomes an educational tool that a beginner can use to form a foundation for further studies. It is also an excellent reading deck that will resonate with the pagan soul.

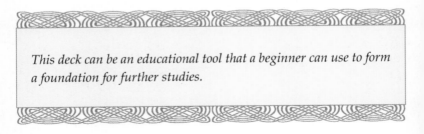

This deck can be an educational tool that a beginner can use to form a foundation for further studies.

Because these cards, the Major Arcana, represent archetypal energies and basic teachings of paganism, when reversed or surrounded by unfavorable cards, their meanings are not changed. Instead, their energy should be read as blocked or stagnant. Generally, if these (or any cards) are reversed, the querent can improve the situation by taking steps to release or unbind the repressed energy.

The first five cards represent very basic core beliefs. These are the essential aspects upon which all else is built. These include The God, the Goddess, the World, the Elements, and the Summerlands.

The second section includes the Wheel of the Year and eight Sabots that make up the pagan calendar.

Our exploration of the Major Arcana ends with the tools and experiences of the practicing pagan, such as initiation, Book of Shadows, and spellcasting.

A Pagan Framework

XXI, The World

One of paganism's most significant tenets is the immanence of the Divine. This means, as we said earlier, that the Divine is in all things and that all things are divine. All things are connected and share sacredness.

This card, called The World, represents the interconnection of all things. Even the goddess and the god are aspects of something larger, a single life force that is unfathomable to us in a complete sense; it transcends thought. The Divine is the entity that is in each of us and in all things,

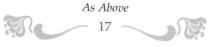

the source of all. The Great Mind, the Universe, or the Great Spirit are other names for the Divine.

Because humans cannot comprehend the fullness of the Divine in a meaningful or practical way and the Divine desires to be in relationship with us, it does what it can to help. Our brains break things down into parts for easier understanding. We tend to think in polarities: light and dark, good and bad, hot and cold, etc. The first inclination of the human mind when considering a being is to determine whether it is male or female. As so, that is the first division of itself that the Divine presents to us, as we will see in the next two cards.

We see all seasons and phases of life connected to and flowing from the feminine Divine and contained within the masculine Divine. Their (the God and Goddess's) essence is in all things.

The idea that we are all one is both our starting place as pagans as well as our goal. The journey is one of moving from an intellectual understanding to an experiential knowing.

Divinatory meaning: *completeness, wholeness, a sense that all is right with the world, feeling connected.*

III, The Empress: The Goddess and IV, The Emperor: The God

The God and the Goddess are the first division of the Divine that we encounter. Even these concepts, the entirety of all that is female and all that is male, are so vast, containing so many possibilities, that we need further compartmentalization. And so, the God and the Goddess become to us like diamonds with hundreds of facets. Each facet shows a different archetypal face. For the God can be a Father, a Sun God, a Wise Old One. The Goddess can be a Mother, a Huntress, a Destroyer. These archetypal images go a long way in helping us understand the complexity of the Great God and Great Goddess.

Showing the Triple Goddess – that is, the Goddess in the form of the Maiden, Mother, and Crone – is one of the most popular depictions, and a very powerful one. It shows, in one image, three main archetypes of the Goddess and also highlights her changeable nature. While the God is associated with the sun and takes about 365 days to go through a cycle, the Goddess is associated with the moon and goes through her cycle in only 28 days. So in this image, we see the variety of the Goddess' forms, power, and gifts.

The God, with his longer cycle, is generally symbolized by one aspect at a time even though he is associated with each of the four seasons. One of the most common images of the God is the Horned God. The aspect is the God in what we would consider his "prime," strong and determined.

These two cards represent the God and Goddess but, as we will see, they both show their aspects in more specific ways in the form of unique deities, making it easier for us to relate to and understand them.

Divinatory meanings
III, The Empress: *Creativity, birth, abundance, fertility*
IV, The Emperor: *Strength, stability, certainty*

I, The Magician: The Elements

Although this card image looks very simple, there is much to be said about the Elements. A solid understanding of the Elements is an important part of the pagan worldview. We'll go into more detail of the nature of the four Elements in the Minor Arcana

THE ELEMENTS

Magic is the intentional use of personal will to partner with nature to create change in the world for the greatest good of all. When we speak of nature in this context, we mean all that exists. Everything that exists is made up of energy. Understanding how each person and thing reflects and responds to energy, the characteristics of energy in general, and the laws governing energetic behavior is the foundation of effective magical practice. All energy comes from the Divine; it is part of and connected to the Divine.

Energy has characteristics based on its elemental make up and on the individual person or thing's expression of its energy. There are also ideas about how energy behaves. Many people use the seven Hermetic Principles as a guide to understanding this behavior.

These principles influence pagan magical rituals and spell work. The principle of mentalism, for example, is reflected in the emphasis placed on clear intent and conscious effort. The principles of correspondence and vibration influence why we use certain tools and ingredients in various spells. The principle of rhythm is acknowledged when we pay attention to the timing of our magic.

There may be some confusion about so-called positive or negative energy. Because all things are part of the Divine, it isn't useful or accurate to think of energy in terms of good and bad. Instead, there

The seven Hermetic Principles

1. The Principle of Mentalism *states that we are all thoughts in the Divine Mind. Because the Divine is immanent, this applies to us...our experience is based on our thoughts. The beginning of magic is based in thought.*

2. The Principle of Correspondence *is the basis of the saying "as above, so below; as below, so above." This relates to the idea of a holographic universe as well as the concept of the immanent Divine; the whole is contained in any part.*

3. The Principle of Vibration *tells us that everything moves and nothing is ever at rest. Everything has its own vibration. Most of us have experienced this, sometimes remarking that we're "getting bad vibes" from a person or situation.*

4. The Principle of Polarity *says that everything is dual and exists as a pair of opposites. Things that seem to oppose each other are really extremes of the same thing.*

5. The Principle of Rhythm *states that everything flows – in and out, up and down, to and fro. Everything has its own tides.*

6. The Principle of Gender *is not about sex but about the concepts of masculinity and femininity. We also think of this as yin and yang. All things have aspects of both.*

7. The Principle of Cause and Effect *seems obvious: every thought and every action has an effect that creates a reaction. Everything that happens has a cause; there is a reason (or more likely several reasons) why it happened.*

is energy that isn't appropriate for a situation or that is no longer serving your highest good.

Divine energy, at least in most pagan practices, is divided into four types: fire, water, air, and earth. These are not literal elements but archetypal and each has its own characteristics. And although they are not actually fire, water, air, or earth, we understand much about their characteristics if we think of what they are named after. For example fire, which is associated with human will, fuels passion, power, and transformation. It warms, protects, activates, and burns. Water, which is associated with human emotions, facilitates healing, dreams, and secrets. It cleans, soothes, provides flexibility, and erodes. Air, which is associated with human intellect, governs logic, truth, and communication. It liberates, provides a cooling breeze, or creates a tempest. Earth, which is associated with the physical body, reigns over manifestation, fertility, and stability. It is heavy, comforting, nurturing, and slow.

As pagans seek to understand the nature of the elements, they usually establish relationships with elementals, creatures that are rather like nature spirits. They embody and watch over the elements. Each element has its own elemental: salamanders for fire, sylphs for air, undines for water, and gnomes for earth.

This card shows both the Elements themselves as well as human hands. In traditional tarot decks, the Aces of each suit are often depicted with a hand holding the suit designator, representing a gift filled with great potential from the Universe. Here the hands represent that but also something more: the ability to work with and direct those energies for conscious co-creation with Universe. This is a very traditional meaning for I, The Magician and it is also the definition of magic: the ability to work with elemental energies to consciously co-create with the Universe.

Divinatory meaning: *skillful use of resources, focused will, insightful understanding of a situation*

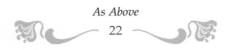

0, The Fool: The Summerlands

Many pagans believe in reincarnation and think of the Summerlands as a beautiful place where the soul goes in between incarnations. Beliefs regarding what occurs in this place and during this time vary widely amongst modern pagans. Some possibilities include the following.

Generally, the Summerlands is considered a place of rest between lives. The soul can find refreshment and perhaps reconnect with loved ones here. Many pagans believe that we pick the lessons we want to experience in each life. The Summerlands provides time to reflect on the lessons selected for the previous life, to consider whether or not they've been learned, and to decide which lessons to experience in the next life. We do not bring our memories of the Summerlands with us into our earthly incarnations.

This image illustrates a scene from the Summerlands, a lovely place were we enjoy ourselves and select the seeds to create our future life. The creation of the next incarnation is represented in this image by the use of light and dark energy. The figure draws the dark energy, which is unformed energy, into itself and transforms it, as represented by the butterflies, into its future life in the form of the sparkling white light opening up before the figure.

Divinatory meaning: *a new life, a fresh start, a journey into the unknown, naiveté.*

X, The Wheel: Wheel of the Year

The Wheel of the Year is an earth-based, nature-centric liturgical year marked by the holidays, called Sabbats, celebrated by pagans. We follow the seasons and the cycles of birth, growth, and death found in nature and serve to deepen our connection with the energies of the earth. As we follow the seasons, we also experience what we call the "meta-myth" of the Great God and Great Goddess. Through these festivals, we acknowledge and honor the many facets of the Divine.

WHEEL OF THE YEAR

Each Sabbat focuses on one spoke in the Wheel and on a particular aspect of the Great God and Great Goddess' story. As we know, in paganism there is no one set of myths or one book of stories. All myths tell the story in different ways. The Sabbats described in the cards below illustrate the meta-myth. That is, the general outline of the story of the God and Goddess, from the birth of the baby God to his eventual sacrifice and death. But most pagans incorporate the pantheon or myths that resonate with them to fill in the details of the story. Since this is a wheel, a circle with no beginning or end, it is challenging to decide where the year logically begins, although many consider Samhain as the ending of an old year and the beginning of a new year.

The festivals are often celebrated by a community or group as well as by individuals in solitary rituals. The communal festivities are more than parties. Observing them is a spiritual and magical act. Each one offers different lessons, teachings, power, and healing. We learn to relate to ourselves, others, and our deities in unique and deeper ways. It is thought that in ancient times these holidays were celebrated as a sort of superstition (or magic, depending on your point of view) that helped insure the continuance of life. We don't really know for sure.

Today we celebrate to strengthen our relationship with nature and to attune to the cycles of the Divine. By participating, whether on a grand, public scale or with a smaller, personal ritual, we help turn the wheel and heal the imbalances that exist in nature due to humankind's abuse of the earth. By not participating, by not connecting with the flow of nature, we are part of the disruption. When we lend our will, our strongest form of energy, to turning the wheel, we connect with the Divine in a very powerful way.

Divinatory meaning: *change is in the air, the next logical step, changing fortunes, repeating cycles*

XVIII, The Moon: Samhain
Samhain (October 31)

During this festival, the Great Goddess reigns in the form of the Crone and the Great God in the form of the Horned God or the Lord of Death. Pagans honor ancestors and prepare for a time of reflection. Some consider Samhain the most important holiday, saying it marks the end of the old year and the beginning of the new year. Because this was the season when weaker animals in flocks were killed and eaten, Samhaim is associated with death in general and the (yearly) death of the God. It is said that on this evening that the veil between the worlds is thin, making it an ideal time for divination and for honoring the ancestors. This holiday prepares us for the dark days ahead.

This card shows a witch honoring the spirits of Samhain and seeking guidance from the ancestors. She accepts the darkness without fear but with respect, knowing that she is strengthening her connection with the Divine.

Divinatory meaning: *darkness, the unknown, reflection and preparation, strong spiritual connections, communication between realms*

XIII, Death: Yule

Winter Solstice or Yule (around December 21)

On the longest night of the year, the Great Mother gives birth to the Sun God and pagans celebrate the return of light to the world. At Samhain, when the God dies, he takes the light with him. After the Winter Solstice, the sun begins to return and so does the God, in the form of a baby. Yule is a joyous celebration of the return of light, life, and warmth.

Yule is also a celebration of faith. The light has not actually begun its return, so it is an act of faith to believe that it will return. The moment of the longest night before the lengthening days is brief, like the moment of death…. It is nearly impossible to pinpoint the exact moment that one thing ends and another begins. Nearly impossible, but that moment does exist. This card shows that moment, when the dead Holly King hands over rulership to the Oak King.

Divinatory meaning: *the end of something, a moment of darkness before the dawn, a crisis of faith, fear of or hope for change.*

XVII, The Star: Imbolc

Imbolc (February 2)

The baby Sun God grows as he is nurtured by the Great Mother. Pagans begin calling to the Goddess, asking her to return from the Underworld. While Yule celebrates the return of the sun, Imbolc rejoices in the first signs of spring, when the snow and ice of winter begin to thaw and new lives begin. Imbolc means "in the belly" and Oimelc means "ewe's milk," signifying a clear connection between this holiday and the lambs soon to be born. During this celebration, witches focus on purification. It is a timing of cleaning things out, both literally and symbolically.

Divinatory meaning: healing, hope, peace, comfort, guidance, direction, a light in the darkness, gentle refreshment.

XIV, Temperance: Ostara

Spring Equinox or Ostara (around March 20)

Pagans celebrate as the world is filled with new life as the Goddess, in the form of the Maiden, returns to the land from the Underworld. Ostara is a playful celebration of spring, new life, fertility. The air is alive with potential. Because this holiday falls on an equinox, balance is an important aspect, but perhaps even more than that, fertility is celebrated. Seasonally-speaking, death and winter are truly conquered and the God and Goddess have returned to the land from the underworld.

The brown bunny (at the Goddesses feet) and the white bunny (in her arms) are a nod to the balance inherent in this holiday and while acknowledging that the days are becoming longer than the nights. Life is becoming more prevalent than death. This Goddess pours her sacred water onto the world, giving it life and color and beauty. She embodies delicate balance and elegant grace. Like an egg shell, that is strong enough to nurture new life but at the right moment is weak enough to be broken through, releasing its contents into the world.

Divinatory meaning: *balance, grace, flowing easily within the world, being at ease in your life, being in the right place at the right time.*

VI, Lovers: Beltane

Beltane (May 1)

The Sun God is no longer a baby, but fully grown. At this festival, the God and Goddess become man and wife and pagans celebrate their union and fertility. This holiday is like the wedding of the God and Goddess. The baby God has grown into manhood, nearing his prime. Since just after Yule, he has been coming into his power. Beltane celebrates their union, their fertility, and all it promises. It is on the opposite side of Samhain on the Wheel of the Year and, like Samhain, this is a time when the veil between the worlds is thin.

As with much of pagan symbolism, the Beltane symbol of the Maypole is obviously sexual. This holiday celebrates virility and the joy of sexual pleasure, and by extension, of life in its prime. For some, this time just before the peak of life, is the sweetest and the best. This card, with its revelers, Maypole, and passionate God and Goddess highlights both the holiday itself and the meaning of the card: the joy and beauty of choosing wisely. When one makes a decision that makes the heart glad, prolific life generally follows.

Divinatory meaning: *following your heart; making a good choice; a happy, healthy partnership; finding a perfect match.*

XIX, The Sun: Litha

Summer Solstice, Midsummer, or Litha (around June 20)

On the longest day of the year, the God, in the form of the Oak King, is in his full power. Pagans celebrate his glory and the promise of abundance of the pregnant Goddess. Although the Goddess is, as always, important, this holiday focuses on the sun and consequently on the God. The first fruits of summer are ripening. The atmosphere is a languid but expectant. People enjoy the sweetness of nature, a foreshadowing of the rich abundance to come.

Litha as well as the Sun card are both relatively simple. In both, there is the sense that everything is pleasant and sweet. The sun is warm, the fruit is sweet, and no one is in a rush. Everyday moments are dripping with pleasure. There is a feeling a success and accomplishment without stress or strife. Even a strong man in his prime, full of potential and plans, finds the time to pet a bunny. Because after this holiday, the days begin to shorten, there is the tiniest hint of melancholy, as the God will face his certain death and the Goddess will withdraw to the Underworld.

Divinatory meaning: *a time of pleasant success, enjoyment of everyday life, happily reaping the first fruits of your efforts.*

XV, The Devil: Lammas

Lammas (August 1)

The first of three harvest festivals, Lammas recognizes the sacrifice of the Oak King to feed the earth. The Holly King begins his reign as father and protector. Thankfulness for the first harvest, represented symbolically by loaves of bread, and acknowledging that everything has a price are important aspects of this holiday. While pagans are grateful for the harvest, they know that it comes with a price – the eventual death of the God and the coming of darkness.

As the end of the growing season draws closer, there is an air of celebration and wild abandon. Games are played, wagers made, and bread and beer enjoyed. The Devil card is often associated with the god Pan, and hence is an appropriate match for this holiday, although the beverage of choice is more often made of grain than grapes. There is almost an "eat, drink, and be merry, for tomorrow we die" sensibility. There is utter enjoyment without thinking about putting anything by for the future.

Divinatory meaning: *enjoyment of the physical world, indulgence or perhaps over-indulgence, taking chances that may pay off or taking risks with too high a price.*

XI, Justice: Mabon

Autumnal Equinox or Mabon (around September 21)

As the days begin to shorten, the Sun God and the Mother Goddess return to the Underworld. Pagans celebrate the bounty of the year as well as prepare for winter. Without modern food preservation techniques or grocery stores, storing enough food for winter had a different urgency, one that we probably cannot imagine. Survival was in the front of everyone's mind and everyone had to work together. At this time of year, prisoners were released and disagreements were set aside. At Mabon, we focus on forgiveness and letting go of unhealthy thoughts and feelings that have settled in our hearts that can fester and turn poisonous.

In this card, Demeter stays on the land for a little longer while her daughter Persephone begins her journey to the Underworld. There is a sense of gratitude for what has been given and a sense of responsibility for what will be required. This is a time to prepare our lives, both mundane and spiritual, for the cold, dark days to come.

Divinatory meaning: *a time of accounting, weighing out the consequences of your actions, making decisions now that will shape your future.*

IX, The Hermit: The Path

Every witch, every pagan, every person for that matter, lives their own life and walks their own path. While there are moments and beliefs that we can share, times when we can help and support each other, when it comes right down to it, our journey is our own. We decide what to do, what to think, what to feel, and what to believe. We determine our values and set our priorities. No matter how entwined our lives are with others, at the day of the day, alone in the woods, we take our own journey; we walk our

THE PATH

own path. Fortunately, when we are alone, focused on our own heart and our own connection with the Divine, that is when we can best hear the Divine's voice and see its guidance. Our path becomes visible and wisdom becomes our companion.

Divinatory meaning: *making your own decisions, seeking guidance from the Divine away from the influence of others, trusting your inner self.*

VIII, Strength: Spellcasting

Magic is focusing the will and working with the Divine energies present to create positive change in the world. Learning to recognize and work with energy is relatively easy. The challenges are controlling our will and on creating positive change. As humans, it seems that part of our lesson on earth is to muster up and properly channel our will, which sometimes seems too weak or too strong. Creating positive change is also difficult. We don't always want what is good for us or for others. Also, it is not always a simple thing to know what is for the greatest good. Managing our will takes practice, discipline,

and patience. Dealing with the question of "greatest good" is eased by maintaining a close connection with the Divine. Once you know how it feels to be in good relationship with the Divine, it is easy to recognize when you are not. That sensitivity can be a great compass.

Divinatory meaning: *mastering yourself, managing resources, creating change, working in harmony with the Divine*

V, The Hierophant: Book of Shadows

Your Book of Shadows serves as your own personal spell book and magical diary. It is a record of your studies, explorations, and conclusions. As you practice, you will synthesize what you read, learn, and experience into your own belief system. In it you will keep track of your rituals, spells, divinations, and meditations. Some practitioners keep separate books for different subjects; others keep everything together in chronological order. Think about how you may use your book and then organize in a way that makes sense with your plans. If your first organizational attempt doesn't feel right, try another until you find the one that works best for you. This Book will form the foundation of your practice and your beliefs. Within its pages you find your own tenets, rules, recipes, devotions, traditions, and goals.

The word hierophant, the name this card traditionally bears, comes from the Greek words ta hiera, meaning "holy" or "sacred" and phainein meaning "to show," "bring to light," or "to make known." But in paganism, no one does this – reveals the sacred – to us. The Divine reveals her/himself. And we make sense of it as we see fit. And so, our Book of Shadows becomes our teacher and our guide

Most of us begin with a blank book. That book holds nothing – nothing except every possibility that exists. Just as we create our future with each moment we live, so we create our personal magical journey with each page of our Book of Shadows that we fill. The world is our classroom. What lessons will manifest and shape your path?

Divinatory meaning: *knowledge, tradition, understanding, beliefs practiced in daily life.*

As Above

VII, The Chariot: Transformation

Our lives are a cycle and have cycles within cycles. Many of these are the natural result of life; we cannot change them, only flow with them or flail against them. The way we experience them can be a transformative experience.

We also create cycles ourselves by the choices we make and the actions we take. And these cycles, the consequences are also life changing. In addition, the choices we make and the thought process by which we arrive at those decisions are also transformative experiences.

As we move through all the co-existing cycles, we create change and we are change. It is an interesting paradox. We exist in the middle of it as the earth exists in both night time and day light.

Divinatory meaning: *change, movement, transformation, conscious reaction.*

XVI, The Tower: Warnings

As mentioned early, there is really no bad energy, only inappropriate energy. And in the same way, there are no bad omens or experiences, but ones that we might consider inconvenient or undesirable, as least in the short term. How can a majestic tree being destroyed by lightning be a positive thing, we wonder. All is one. The tree, the lightning, and the fire are all part of the Divine. The moon, a shadowy light that conceals more than it reveals, reminds us that we do not always understand the reasons for everything that happens around us.

These things, these traumas, these disasters – for to us, they are those things – do happen. We may not understand why, but we are sometimes given a portent, a warning, so that we may be prepared.

Divinatory meaning: *trouble ahead, a sudden and unexpected event, seemingly senseless destruction.*

XII, The Hanged Man: The Circle

A Circle is a sacred space that you create for any spiritual work that you do. A sacred space can be created anywhere. Think of it as a metaphorical cauldron. A cauldron is a place that holds ingredients, keeping what you want all in one place while making sure unwanted materials do not mix in. On another level, it is also a place of transformation. Your sacred space is your temple where you work with the energy you invite in and form a boundary that separates you from unwanted energy. While in your space, you expect revelations and experiences; you expect transformation. These expectations are a form of intent. Creating a sacred space is important but not difficult.

THE CIRCLE

1. Cleanse the area

Students of Feng Shui know the importance of an orderly environment. Being in a space free from clutter and distractions allows energy to flow unimpeded and aids in your ability to focus. Energetic cleaning methods include smudging the area with sage or ringing a bell around the area. The sage purifies the area. The bell is said to break up stagnant energy and is usually done before smudging.

2. Gather your tools

After the area is clear, make sure you have everything you need for the work you intend to do. For meditation, this will likely be very little, just your journal and your focus object, if you are using one. For rituals and spell work, you will have more items in your circle.

3. Ground

Ground yourself by sitting or standing in the area where you intend to create your space. Take three long, slow deep breaths, feel-

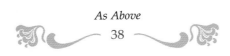

ing calmness entering you with each inhalation and tension and distractions leaving you with each exhalation. Imagine that a root is growing out of the soles of your feet (if your feet are flat on the floor) or base of your spine (if you are sitting) traveling toward the earth. Feel it enter the earth. Take three more slow breaths, imagining the stability of the earth entering your body with each inhalation and all unnecessary energy leaving you, returning to the earth where it will be grounded and stored until needed again, with each exhalation.

4. Define the space

While still in the center of your space, extend your dominant arm and your index finger as if pointing. Imagine energy running through your grounding root, up through your feet, legs, and spine, down your arm, and coming out of your fingertip. Aim the energy to the parameter of your circle. Direct the energy in a clockwise motion until you have completed tracing the circumference of your space. As your create this boundary say (silently or out loud) something like, "With this energy, I cast this circle, a space beyond space, a time beyond time, a place of transformation."

When you are finished, stand in the center, as described in step 4, and trace your circle counter-clockwise saying something like, "With this energy, I release this circle and return to ordinary time and space." Because you have worked with intensely focused energy, be sure to ground yourself once more, releasing all unneeded energy back into the earth.

Divinatory meaning: *creating a safe and clean environment, setting boundaries, focusing exclusively on the spiritual for a time.*

XX, Judgement: Initiation

Everyone walks their own path. And everyone hears their spiritual call in their own way. For the witch, once she hears the call of the Divine, of the Goddess, and of the God, she commits herself to honoring them. It is like the old chants that medieval monks sang, with a call and a response. This card is about this relationship, this agreement. We are called to a specific life and we promise to live our believes has best we can. Mostly, we promise to stay in right relationship with the Divine so we can hear the needs and guidance of our deities with the same clarity with which we heard our original 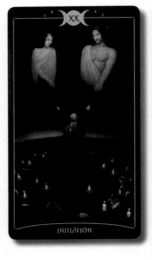 call and so that we can answer with the same passionate intensity.

Divinatory meaning: spiritual calling, living with a higher purpose, leaving an old way of living.

II, The High Priestess: Wisdom

In Paganism, we are each our own High Priestess (or Priest). In a sense, this what we strive for. Indeed, for many tarot readers, this is the card with which they most identify. Unlike traditional tarot decks where the High Priestess represents non-rational/non-logical sources of knowledge, this Priestess represents Wisdom. The yin and the yang. The athame and the chalice. The magical combination of opposites: intellect (as in rational/logic thinking) and intuition. When these two aspects work together, we can find true wisdom. Again, this is the alchemical balance most tarot readers seek: combining  an intellectual understanding of the tarot with intuitive responses to the symbols and images in the cards.

Divinatory meaning: *very simply: wisdom, combining intelligence and intuition, seeking the whole truth.*

The Divinatory meanings of the Major Arcana in numerical order

0, The Fool: *A new life, a fresh start, a journey into the unknown, naiveté.*

I, The Magician: *skillful use of resources, focused will, insightful understanding of a situation.*

II, The High Priestess: *wisdom, combining intelligence and intuition, seeking the whole truth.*

III, The Empress: *Creativity, birth, abundance, fertility.*

IV, The Emperor: *Strength, stability, certainty.*

V, The Hierophant: *Knowledge, tradition, understanding, beliefs practiced in daily life.*

VI, The Lovers: *Following your heart; making a good choice; a happy, healthy partnership; finding a perfect match.*

VII, Transformation: *Change, movement, transformation, conscious reaction.*

VIII, Strength: *Mastering yourself, managing resources, creating change, working in harmony with the Divine.*

IX, The Hermit: *Making your own decisions, seeking guidance from the Divine away from the influence of others, trusting your inner self.*

X, The Wheel: *Change is in the air, the next logical step, changing fortunes, repeating cycles.*

XI, Justice: *A time of accounting, weighing out the consequences of your actions, making decisions now that will shape your future.*

XII, The Hanged Man: *Creating a safe and clean environment, setting boundaries, focusing exclusively on the spiritual for a time.*

As Above

XIII, Death: *The end of something, a moment of darkness before the dawn, a crisis of faith, fear of or hope for change.*

XIV, Temperance: *grace, flowing easily within the world, being at ease in your life, being in the right place at the right time.*

XV, The Devil: *Enjoyment of the physical world, indulgence or perhaps over-indulgence, taking chances that may pay off or taking risks with too high a price.*

XVI, The Tower: *Trouble ahead, a sudden and unexpected event, seemingly senseless destruction.*

XVII, The Star: *Healing, hope, peace, comfort, guidance, direction, a light in the darkness, gentle refreshment.*

XVIII, The Moon: *Darkness, the unknown, reflection and preparation, strong spiritual connections, communication between realms.*

XIX, The Sun: *A time of pleasant success, enjoyment of everyday life, happily reaping the first fruits of your efforts.*

XX, Judgement: *Spiritual calling, living with a higher purpose, leaving an old way of living.*

XXI, The World: *completeness, wholeness, a sense that all is right with the world, feeling connected.*

Suggested Reading List

Wicca for Beginners by Thea Sabin
Wicca: A Guide for the Solitary Practitioner by Scott Cunningham
The Inner Temple of Witchcraft by Christopher Penczak
The Outer Temple of Witchcraft by Christopher Penczak

The Four Elements

The four suits of the Minor Arcana represent the four Elements: Fire, Water, Air, and Earth. As you read through the sections below, you will be introduced to the Elements in some detail and through various facets. The Elements themselves are archetypal, like the cards of the Major Arcana, and are expressed and experienced in many different ways. The Elements are often associated with Elemental Beings. In this deck, the Fire suit features salamanders, the suit of Water has undines, sylphs dart through the suit of Air, and gnomes are at home in the suit of Earth.

While each suit has its own characteristics, there are some shared characteristics. The suits of Fire and Air are naturally active and often described as masculine. Water and Earth are passive or receptive, and are usually spoken of as feminine. Consequently, we often use the appropriate pronoun when discussing the Elementals, although the idea of gender is metaphoric rather than actual.

The Court Cards

Traditionally populated by Kings and Queens, Knights and Pages, the court cards in this deck pay homage to the four elements that we work with and the faces of the Goddess in her aspects of Maiden, Mother, and Crone. In these cards, we can learn more about the elements as well as about the many, many ways that the Goddess manifests in our lives, through situations, other people, and ourselves. When interpreting these cards in a reading, keep that in mind. They can represent the Element or Goddess, other people, or yourself, even though the divinatory meanings will be written from the point of view of the Element or the Goddess. If you are familiar with traditional tarot decks, the Element cards in this deck function more like Aces in other decks in that they represent the element in its pure form.

Like the Major Arcana, theses court cards represent archetypal energies and the faces of the Goddess, when reversed or surrounded by unfavorable cards, their meanings are not changed. Instead, their energy is represented as blocked or stagnant. Remember, if these cards are reversed, the querent can improve the situation by taking steps to release or unbind the repressed energy.

Fire

The salamander has long been associated with this suit. He is at home in the heat and brightness created by fire. In addition, he carries within him a seed of fire. Surrounded by it and filled with it, he is the essence of the element. The element of Fire is passion, creativity, spirituality, energy, and, perhaps most importantly, of our will. It is the element we incorporate when we want to pump up the volume, light off fireworks, or loose ourselves in our work. It is assertive, even aggressive. Powerful. Dangerous. Exciting.

One of the easiest and most effective ways to incorporate the Element of Fire into your magical work, ritual practices, or spiritual observances is through the use candles. Candles can be used as a focal point for meditation. To more specifically focus your intent by selecting certain colors of candles to light, by anointing your candles with specially chosen oil, or by carving runes, symbols, or words into your candles.

The **Element of Fire** brings an influx of fiery energy to the situation. It is there for you to use, if you can, or to counter-balance, if need be.

The **Maiden of Fire** lights a single candle. She gives, as a gift, the first spark of inspiration.

The **Mother of Fire** tends the fire. She nurtures the gift of fire within your life and helps it grow.

The **Crone of Fire** blows out the flame. There is a time and a season for everything. She is here to usher in the ending, the dying of the fire.

Suggested Reading List
Candle Magic by Richard Webster

ELEMENTAL OF FIRE

MAIDEN OF FIRE

MOTHER OF FIRE

CRONE OF FIRE

As Above

Air

Lithe and quick, sylphs are often associated with air. Air can be light and refreshing as a breeze. It can be strong and quick, like a spring wind that raises a kite. It can also be powerful and destructive, like a tornado. Keeping this in mind, we might remember that our words and our thoughts, also associated with the Element of Air, share these qualities. We can utter words that destroy or lift someone up. We can think thoughts the sooth our mind or work ourselves up into a frenzy. It is really quite amazing how powerful invisible things like thoughts and air can be.

In addition to what we think, this Element represents how we think. That is, our world view, philosophy, or outlook on life. World views can be simple, as in yes or no, black or white – ideas that can be expressed or decided with a pendulum. Philosophies or ideas can be extremely layered and complex, like a tarot reading. The Element of Air is changeable and can be swift, sharp, and intelligent or just as easily gentle, uplifting, and refreshing. Turn to the Element of Air when you want to solve a problem, learn the truth, and communicate with someone.

The **Element of Air** blows a bit of fresh insight into a situation. There is the potential for it to help cut to the chase and resolve things or add layers of complication. Be aware of it and use as best you can.

The **Maiden of Air** shares a song with the creatures of the air. She encourages intuitive, spontaneous, and joyful communication.

The **Mother of Air** writes books and creates language. She builds bridges with words and ideas, helping you communicate more effectively.

The **Crone of Air** closes the book. There are some things that you are not meant to know at this time. For now, let it go.

ELEMENTAL OF AIR

MAIDEN OF AIR

MOTHER OF AIR

CRONE OF AIR

As Above

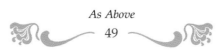

Water

Although the Element of Water is considered passive, it often feels very powerful. Represented by undines (also known has water spirits), the Element of Water is associated with emotions, feelings, and relationships. Like Air, Water is by turns gentle and powerful. As a spring shower, it cleanses and brings forth new life. As a downpour, it brings floods, mudslides, and destruction. The physical presence of water in our lives can change how we feel. After a hard day, a cool shower can renew us. Steady, monotonous rain falling from a gray sky can lower our mood and encourage introspection or melancholy.

Invoke the Element of Water when you want to feel or express love, joy, happiness, sadness, or mourning. Water enhances artistic expression, healing, and connections with others. Without Water life is flat and bland. This Element helps us flow through life, deftly and effortlessly finding its way through and around anything in its way.

The **Element of Water** lets you know that there are plenty of emotions involved in the situation. Anything could happen and anyone of them can turn from positive to negative at a moment's notice. You will have to manage things carefully – but if you do, you'll generate a lot of useful energy.

The **Maiden of Water** plays with a dolphin and splashes in the water. She promises a fresh, youthful approach, filled with positive energy.

The **Mother of Water** brings down the rains. She nourishes the relationships and feelings that are needed for life to flourish.

The **Crone of Water** puts some water in a bottle. She knows that there will come a difficult time when a dear memory will be needed.

ELEMENTAL OF WATER

MAIDEN OF WATER

MOTHER OF WATER

CRONE OF WATER

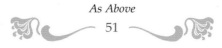

As Above

Earth

The tangible world – our mother and our teacher. Solid. Practical. The manifestation of our thoughts and feelings. The Earth supplies food for all parts of the human experience: body, mind, and soul; it engages and delights all of our senses. Earth gives physical form to our spiritual journey and helps us connect concretely to the Wheel of Life. From the promise of birth and Spring, through blossoming, fruition, and harvest, to the final pause of death and decay until the cycle begins anew, we see and experience the cycle on the physical as well as spiritual planes.

We focus on the Element of Earth when we seek security, boundaries, sensuality, growth, abundance, and pleasure. Earth provides stability and grounds us. It provides us strength and gives us somewhere to release unneeded or inappropriate energy. Earth is a very comfortable elemental. Be careful not to get too comfortable or stagnation may set in.

The **Element of Earth** is a sure sign of prosperity, abundance, and manifestation. The energy surrounding and filling the situation is solid and stable. This bodes well for completing any task, but take care to keep other energy flowing or the whole situation could collapse in a pile of stagnation.

The **Maiden of Earth** takes her place among the new blossoms of the field. She brings a sense of lightness and gratitude, a joyful appreciation and celebration of everyday blessings.

The **Mother of Earth** takes her place as Mother Nature, providing a rich harvest. She nourishes our bodies and our souls with the best of Her creation.

The **Crone of Earth** lays the Earth to rest. Even the Earth must regenerate, and there is a time for everything in this life, including death.

ELEMENTAL OF EARTH

MAIDEN OF EARTH

MOTHER OF EARTH

CRONE OF EARTH

As Above

The Minor Arcana

These cards combine the traditional tarot correspondences of elemental energies with useful information and techniques that may prove useful to the pagan practitioner. The Suit of Fire, also known as Wands, shows the planets and teaches about astrological influences. The Suit of Air, also know as Swords, is about communication and hence shows different ways we communicate with the Divine, or divination. The Suit of Water, also known as Cups, focuses on relationships and is represented by one way we experience relationship with the Divine – through the faces of the Goddess. The Suit of Earth, also known as Pentacles, explores the wondrous ways the Divine reveals itself in the physical world.

Unlike the Major Arcana and the Court Cards in this deck, the Minor cards in this deck have a spectrum of meanings and include both a regular meaning as well as a shadow meaning, which can be used if the card appears reversed.

The Suit of Fire

In astrology, the planets are considered the main active forces. They have been described as actors. Astrological signs are roles the various actors can play. The houses are the scenes or setting in which the actors play those roles. Because the planets are the active force, the energy and the drive behind all that happens astrologically, they are the best aspect to represent the suit of Fire.

The influence of the planets affects us whether we wish it to or not. However, we can understand these influences and, to some extent, learn to employ them. In fact, some of the planets' energies are easier to direct than others. Some are more unwieldy, but the better we understand them, the easier time we'll have experiencing them. Generally speaking, the closer the planets are to the Sun, the easier it is manage their energy. Hence, we tend to have more ability to use the power of the Ace, Two, Three, and Four. These planets' influence are also shorter lived than the outer planets. The Five, Six, Seven, Eight, Nine, and Ten become increasingly independent with longer-term ramifications.

Most of the planets are named after and symbolized by aspects of the God. In this sense, the suit of Fire is a counterpart to the suit of Water, which represents aspects of the Goddess. While the Sun and the Stars find their way into the suit of Fire, the Moon does not. Instead, you'll find the Moon and her aspects depicted in the court cards. The planet Earth, as well, is not part of the suit of Fire. We find the aspects and powers of the Earth described in its very own suit.

The cards in the suit of Fire introduce basic astrological concepts that can be used when determining timing for magic, divination, meditation, or rituals. Ways to utilize this information can be found at the end of this chapter. In addition, when these cards appear in readings, they represent energy that is at play in a situation or can give advice about what sort of energy or activity to act on.

Ace of Fire: The Sun

There is a saying about people who are very self-centered; we say that such people think that they are "the center of the universe." In the case of the Sun, it is somewhat true, for this heavenly body is the center of the solar system.

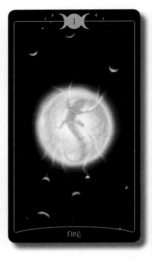

The power of the Sun keeps the planets in their orbits. Everything is, therefore, directly related to the Sun. Besides being an intense gravitational provider, the Sun is the solar system's source of heat and light. Its existence is defined by its ability to shine.

Astrologically, the Sun highlights what area we wish desire to excel at. It identifies our core personality, shapes our sense of self. The Sun shines a light on who we think we are.

The Ace of Fire represents strong personal energy at work. This card is something we wish very much to do not just well but excellently. It is a hotly burning desire that can be directed and used to light a project, large or small, and has the potential to create glorious fireworks, or even just delightful sparks.

The shadow side of this card represents a more dangerous or perhaps only disappointing outcome. Ego, self-centeredness, selfishness are possible. There is the danger of energy burning too hot too quickly and thus burning out either without any useful effect or with a destructive, scorching result.

Two of Fire: Mercury

The Roman god called Mercury was known for, among other things, delivering messages between gods, goddesses, and mortals.

Astrologically, this Mercury deals with how we think and reason as well as how we communicate, including writing, speaking, and listening. By extension, it also governs how we gather and process data.

The excuse "oh, Mercury is retrograde" is common amongst people who talk about astrology. When a planet is retrograde, it appears to be moving backwards across the sky – rather like a tarot card being reversed. When Mercury is in retrograde people are advised to not buy electronics, to back up their computers, to not sign contracts of any sort, or to start anything new because communications are bound to be problematic. Instead, this retrograde energy is considered best for reviewing work already finished. Also, it is said that during a Mercury retrograde, mistakes made in the past can come back to haunt us or that we may hear from people we haven't heard from for a while.

In addition to communication, Mercury also governs short journeys, siblings, co-workers, neighbors, and agreements.

The Two of Fire represents the importance of communication. Either there is something that must be said or something that must be heard. The surrounding cards will help identify which way the communication needs to be flowing and with whom.

The shadow side of this card indicates miscommunication that is causing a significant problem pertinent to the situation – in other words, it represents Mercury in retrograde.

As Above

Three of Fire: Venus

The goddess Venus is almost universally equated with love and romance, beauty and pleasure. She also governs creativity, talents of all sorts, and art.

As an astrological player, Venus is true to her image and certainly represents love, partnerships, and marriage. Those, however, are just one facet of Venus's energy. At her most basic, she represents attraction. Both what we are attracted to and what we attract to ourselves. Looking at this idea in terms of the Law of Attraction, we draw toward us and are drawn toward what we value and what we desire.

The Three of Fire denotes the energy of attraction, whether to another person, to an ideal, or to an item. We can see by this card and those surrounding it how the attraction itself affects the situation. In addition, the nature of the thing desired or value may be revealed.

The shadow side of this card indicates revulsion, denial of attraction, or attraction thwarted.

Four of Fire: Mars

Mars is a warrior, known for bravery and action. This god may very well be the most literal representation of fire in this suit, for he is moved to swift action by fiery passion.

Astrologically, Mars shows energy, courage, confidence, and strength. This is the energy that helps us stand up for ourselves, to follow adventure, and be spontaneous. Mars's power comes from the fire that burns in our gut. It is both formidable and dangerous, moving from defensive protection to aggressive attack with surprising ease. If not controlled or channeled appropriately this energy can lead to violence, accidents, or cruelty.

The Four of Fire shows the desire for action. The situation is fraught with energy that is powerful and fast moving. There is the need for courage, confidence, and possibly defensiveness.

The shadow side of this card represents misdirected energy and the danger of extreme and inappropriate aggression, anger, and violence.

Five of Fire: Jupiter

Jupiter is like everyone's favorite uncle – generous, fun, and charming. He is known as the Great Benefactor. He always surrounded by a crowd who bask in the favors flowing in his wake.

Jupiter is a large planet and, astrologically, packs a big punch. Jupiter represents expansion, growth, progress, and abundance. Although often associated with material good luck, Jupiter also blesses our lives in other ways by bringing joy, faith, inspiration, and understanding. All of these experiences usually lead to a healthy optimism that encourages us to expand our worlds with new experiences such as traveling, networking, or taking classes.

The Five of Fire in a reading lets us know that good things are afoot and to enjoy them. Whatever lucky break comes our way is a gift, which can be enjoyed for its own sake alone…or it can be parlayed into something even greater. Use the happiness and optimism that the gift generates to create even more good luck by seeking out even more experiences.

The shadow side of this card suggests wasting such gifts, ingratitude, or blowing something out of proportion.

Six of Fire: Saturn

While Jupiter is the life of the party, Saturn's reputation is less favorable. Known for challenges, restrictions, and hard work, Saturn's benefits are often overlooked.

Saturn rules our ambitions, goals, career, achievements, and long term plans. These are all worthy things that often shape our lives to a significant degree. With achievements come kudos and recognition, but with Saturn these are all hard won. And it is in the winning of them that Saturn's true gifts given. Our journey toward realizing our ambitions is filled with serious choices, including how we deal with authority figures and obstacles. We confront structures and restrictions and must determine how we face them, overcome them, or work within them. Through this we gain experience and wisdom. Life lessons are taught and learned...or repeated.

The Six of Fire brings a conservative, serious energy. Situations must be reviewed and analyzed and decisions made with calculating precision, for what happens now will determine future trends. Much can be won, but not without a cost.

The shadow side of this card indicates the building of walls and retreat. The fear of failure overwhelms the desire to succeed.

Seven of Fire: Uranus

Uranus is the Crazy Genius of the skies. While he brings shocks and surprises, they are usually, in the long run, exciting and beneficial.

When Uranus decides to make its presence known, it is usually by way of sudden big changes, sometimes brought on by radical, impulsive behavior or just as likely brought on by no apparent cause. The events heralded by Uranus serve to break us out of ruts and inspire our inner genius. Rules are broken willy-nilly and originality and insight ensue. Freed from bonds of stagnation, boundaries, and ennui, independence, innovation, and idealism are the new normal.

The Seven of Fire promises exciting times. We should be ready to expect the unexpected from life and from ourselves. And in this case, do not expect the surrounding cards to provide much detail about the particulars. That's the point of this experience…not knowing what's coming.

The shadow side of this card shows extremely impulsive behavior, radical ideas, and a desire for rebellion that will lead to regret.

Eight of Fire: Neptune

No matter what chaos ensues, Neptune stands calmly in the middle of it all, confident, somehow in control, and rather enjoying the ride.

There is a saying about magic being done with "smoke and mirrors." Neptune is the master of smoke and mirrors and most of his magic focuses on the mind. His energy covers the world with a blanket of romance and glamour. Beguiling mists cover the mundane and inspire the mind to dream or trick it into believing illusions. In this altered state induced by Neptune's charms, the mind relaxes, logic blurs, and synapses make new connections, allowing a welling up of psychic tendencies and letting flow the feelings of compassion, sensitivity, and tolerance.

The Eight of Fire lulls us into daydreams and fantasies. Logic takes a backseat as our soul craves mystery and illusion. Once the mind is quieted and open, we begin to accept and then embrace the possibility of dreams coming true. And Neptune knows that belief is the first to step toward creation.

The shadow side of this card represents delusions, deception, and secrecy. The dreams in this case are more like nightmares and often lead to self-destructive behavior.

Nine of Fire: Pluto

Some say that the only absolutes in life are death and taxes. Pluto reigns over these infamous aspects of the human experience. He does so with cool composure and promises.

Astrologically, whether given status as a planet or not, Pluto governs those things in life that absolutely have to happen. As god of the Underworld, it is fitting that Pluto is associated with death, which leads to transformation and renewal. Really, Pluto is not so much a dispenser of death as he is a surgeon, helping us dispose of situations that are completely played out and shedding anything that no longer serves us. Pluto also deals with issues of sex, power, and control, making sure we know when these are appropriate and necessary to pursue and when it is time to let go. Although the experiences of Pluto are often hard, painful, or even terrifying, the rewards are vast: a renewal of life and spirit, psychological and personal growth, wisdom, the ability to transcend adversity.

The Nine of Fire heralds the inevitable. Unlike the Seven of Fire, the events of the Nine are often not a surprise. More often, we see them coming, we know we should prepare, but we resist. The changes Pluto promises are usually difficult and ones we'd rather forego. While that is not possible, there is, at least, the promise of riches at the end of the journey.

The shadow side of this card shows a strong and dangerous denial of Pluto's events. Like the repressed shadow self, these repressed feelings can lead to explosive and unstable actions, which will not only delay the inevitable but often make it more difficult.

As Above

Ten of Fire: Stars

The Stars in night sky hold so much meaning for humans. We wish upon them, we use them to hold our stories, and we navigate by them.

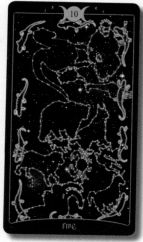

Astrology, the stars play nearly the same functions. As constellations, they represent the signs of the zodiac, which, remember, are the roles the actors (planets) play. They represent the people we wish to be or characteristics we dream of having. They tell us who we are. They help guide us through life.

There is some element of fate associated with stars, as if our futures were all written out across the skies. But that's not quite right. The stars are more like a dealer in a game of poker. We are given a hand of cards and we can play that hand however we like. It is an odd juxtaposition: the role of fate simply serves to highlight the necessity of our choosing how to respond. It demands us to engage our freewill.

The Ten of Fire indicates that the events in question are cannot be changed and that there is a role that must be fulfilled or an action that must be taken. The actions we take in the face of unalterable facts define our nature and shape our character.

The shadow side of this card doesn't change the facts of the matter but instead indicates that we cannot see the stars, we have lost our focus, and feel directionless.

Magical Timing

Just as the gods, goddesses, and elements bring different energy to magical work, every moment in time has its own energy. Using just a basic understanding of astrology can help you pick times that will strengthen your work because the flow of energy will support what you do, not work against it. Magical timing can be very precise, with calculations narrowing down a window for a specific type of magic to a few minutes. However, most of us, for various reasons, use a more generalized approach. Realistically, narrowing down an ideal time to a few moments would make it very difficult for most people to practice at all.

For most of us, paying attention to three basic factors is generally enough to give a beneficial time range. These factors are the phase of the moon, which astrological the Moon is in, and the day of the week. If finding a time that includes optimal aspects for each of these three factors proves difficult, try this order of priorities: first, the moon phase; secondly, the sign that the moon is in; and finally, the day of the week. There are always exceptions. For example, many people consider Sunday a good day for any type of magic. However, if time is of the essence, it is better to do your work than not do it, regardless of timing.

Throughout the course of its twenty-eight day cycle, the moon goes through four main phases: full, waning, dark (or new), and waxing. These phases refer to the way the moon appears based on the light reflected off its surface. The moon itself, of course, doesn't change size. The moon phases correspond to various manifestations of the Triple Goddess. The waxing and waning moons are the Maiden. The full moon is the Mother. The dark moon is the Crone.

A **waning moon** begins the moment after the moon reaches full. As the moon wanes, it becomes smaller each night. The energy of a waning moon is used for banishing. A spell for starting a weight-

As Above

loss or debt-reduction plan works well during a waning moon. Use this energy to boost a spell for anything you want to weaken or eliminate from your life.

A **waxing moon** begins the moment after a dark moon and the moon appears to grow each night. This energy is perfect for anything you want to increase or attract into your life. Spells for a new job, romance, or physical health benefit from this energy.

The **full moon** is one of great magical power, when the moon (and by association, the goddess) is at her strongest and brightest. Astrologically speaking, the energy is said to be effective three days before and after the actual date of the full moon. As you can see there is a substantial difference between a waning and waxing moon. So, even though the energy of a full moon is considered strongest three days before and after, do be careful on the timing. To use the energy of a waxing moon, for example, do your work before the moon hits full.

The **dark or new moon** energy is similar to that of the waning moon, but stronger. It is particularly favored for shadow work, anger issues, or breaking bad habits.

Determining if the moon is waxing or waning is easy, if you can locate it in the night sky. For the northern hemisphere, the moon looks like a "D" (that is, the rounded, convex side is on the right) when it is waxing. It looks like a "C" (that is, the rounded, convex side) is on the left when it is waning. It is the opposite for the southern hemisphere.

No matter what phase the moon is in, it is always in one of the astrological signs. The twelve signs are divided into four groups that happen to coincide with the four elements. Gemini, Libra, and Aquarius are air signs. Aries, Leo, and Sagittarius are fire signs. Cancer, Scorpio, and Pisces are water signs. Taurus, Virgo, and Capricorn are earth signs. The sign the moon is in

flavors the energy that it emits. Spells, for example, about seeking a promotion benefit from the fire signs. Relationship spells are better served by the water signs rather than air signs. Prosperity spells are enhanced by the energy of earth signs. In addition to their elemental attributes, each sign has its own particular energy. Becoming familiar with them will help add more precision to your choices (another good reason to learn a little astrology).

Most calendars show at least the full and new moon dates, and so the waxing and waning phases can be deduced from that information. Use an astrological calendar to know what sign the moon is in. These can be purchased or found online for free.

Each day of the week is governed by a planet. The planet lends its energy to magical timing. This is a simple and useful technique for magical timing and doesn't require a special calendar.

The sun rules **Sunday** and bestows the beneficial effects of success, power, and harmony to any spell. If you cannot decide which day will best suit your work, pick Sunday.

The moon watches over **Monday.** This mysterious energy aids in transformation, intuition, psychic abilities, emotions, and the removal of illusions.

Fiery Mars takes charge of **Tuesday**. Tap into this energy when you need courage, power, victory, protection, or strength.

Mercury reigns over **Wednesday** and helps with any kind of work dealing with communication, intellect, creativity, or travel.

Beneficent Jupiter's power is available on **Thursdays**. The planet of expansion, it is very well suited for spells for finances, prosperity, confidence, happiness, and plain old good luck.

Venus, the only feminine planet represented here, holds sway on **Fridays**. This energy will enhance any work for love, romance, beauty, art, friendship, or selp-help.

Stern Saturn guides **Saturday**'s energy. Use it when focusing on lessons, hard work, goals, insight, protection, and identity issues.

Theoretically speaking, putting these three elements together is not difficult. Ideal circumstances for a love spell might be a Friday when the moon is waxing in Pisces. A prosperity spell would be enhanced on a Thursday during a waxing moon in Taurus. Spell work for a weight loss program gains momentum if done on a Saturday during a waning moon in Aries. However, it can be frustrating trying to find the absolute perfect time. Don't fret, then, if all aspects are not ideal. Prioritize and get as close as you can.

Suggested Reading List
Astrology for Beginners by Joann Hampar
Llewellyn's Complete Book of Astrology by Kris Brandt
Llewellyn's Astrological Calendar or Astrological Pocket Planner

The Suit of Air

Throughout human history, many people have sought the direction and guidance from a source outside themselves. This source has had many names: God, Goddess, Oracle, Great Spirit, or simply the Universe. And just as our Great God and Great Goddess have numerous names and aspects, so there are many ways to connect with the Divine. At its heart, divination is just that: connection with the Divine. Because the suit of Air is traditionally associated with communication, ways of thinking, and truth, the cards in this suit explore various ways we communicate with our Divine.

When we divine, we are seeking answers and guidance. The type of information we want or the question we have can determine the method of divination we choose. Each one has its own strengths. The more we learn about them, the better choices we can make about which to use in any situation. The more we practice them, the more comfortable, confident, and skilled we become.

The cards in the suit of Air not only introduce various forms of divination. In a reading, they also give information about the type of communication, worldview, or truths pertinent to the situation.

Suggested Reading List
Divination for Beginners by Scott Cunningham
I Ching for Beginners by Mark McElroy
Palm Reading for Beginners by Richard Webster
Pendulum Magic for Beginners by Richard Webster
A Practical Guide to the Runes by Lisa Peschel
Tarot for Beginners by Barbara Moore
Meditation for Beginners by Stephanie Clement
Dreams and What They Mean to You by Migene Gonzalez-Wippler
Animal Omens by Victoria Hunt
Familiar Spirits by Donald Tyson

Ace of Air: Dreams

While it is true that science admittedly knows very little about sleep and dreams, it is also true that dreams often provide messages and revelations and even prophecies. For the most part, dreaming is a passive activity. The dreams are received, it seems, as a gift from the Divine. Whether a dream leaves us feeling excited and renewed or frightened and shaken, we are compelled to seek a message from it, to interpret it. It is thought that while the conscious mind is relaxed, the subconscious, or perhaps the God or Goddess, can communicate via dream images.

Dreaming is generally considered a passive activity. However, there are techniques that can be employed to encourage dreams, to remember dreams, and even to use dreams to work through problems or discover truths. Dreams that are particularly frightening, we call nightmares. Nightmares can sometimes impart messages or wisdom, but not always. However, sometimes they are just bad dreams brought on by anxiety or worry. They let us know we are stressed, but often don't provide helpful advice beyond highlighting the source or the anxiety.

Before sleep, meditating and burning certain incense or herbs, such as angelica or mugwort, can encourage dreams, as can petitioning the Divine. Preparing the mind, inviting dreams, and setting the intention to remember them, will help increase dream recall. Keeping a dream journal and pencil by the bed is also helpful, to record dreams in the morning or even in the middle of the night. A few words scribbled in the dark can often help trigger the memory of the whole dream, or at least the part that felt important at the time.

As Above

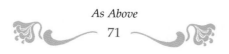

Lucid dreaming is the active type of dreaming. The dreamer is aware of being in a dream and can act and interact within the dream environment. Using this technique opens up many doors and possibility. The reading list below gives a suggestion for a good starting point.

The Ace of Air represents direct Divine guidance. The Universe wishes to provide information, to give it freely, as a gift. However, we must be receptive and cultivate a quiet mind or the gift is lost to us. Settle down, quit striving, and just receive.

The shadow side of this card indicates nightmares that, while powerful, do not empower. Dwelling on them serves no purpose, for they have no lessons to teach or wisdom to impart.

Two of Air: Pendulum

Life is complicated. Many times answers are not simple and situations are not black and white. In order to find the truth of the matter, we plumb the layers and convulsions, looking for patterns, trying to find the path in the woods. However, there are times when things are not complicated. Sometimes the answer is simply "yes" or "no."

Most forms of divination are more suited for the nuanced situations that fill most of our days. In fact, they are so well-suited for those times that they are nearly useless for obtaining clear and easy answers. A pendulum, however, is useful for only the most basic of questions: "this" or "that," "yes" or "no."

A pendulum is a very simple device and can easily be made. It consists of a thread or tiny chain with a lightweight on the end. Lovely pendulums with fancy weights made of metal or precious stones can be purchased. There are even pendulums with tips that open, revealing a tiny receptacle that can hold herbs, oils, or tiny bits of paper. However, as nice as these are, a makeshift pendulum can be devised from a length of threads and a paperclip or employing a necklace chain with a pendant on it.

To use a pendulum, hold the end of the thread or chain in your dominant hand. Rest your elbow on a table or flat surface, letting the pendulum hang straight down. With your feet flat against the floor, center and ground yourself. This is a very important part of working with a pendulum, for you want to be tapped in to the flow of the earth with a very strong connection. Once you are grounded, close your eyes for a few moments thinking about your question. When you feel the time is

As Above

right, open your eyes and observe the pendulum to determine your answer.

Questions that work well with a pendulum are ones that can be answered either "yes" or "no." Questions about choosing between two possibilities also work well. Before using your pendulum, though, you will need to determine how your pendulum responds to you, as it is not always the same for everyone. Do this by asking a series of yes/no questions that you already know the answer to. Keep track of which way the pendulum swings in response to "yes" answers and "no" answers. After establishing consistency, you will know how your pendulum works with your energy. For example, "yes" might be indicated by swinging vertically and "no" horizontally, with an "uncertain" or "unknown" shown by the pendulum moving in a circle.

If you think your question should be easily and clearly answered with a pendulum but find that it is not, that is, if the answer is "uncertain/unknown," try using another from of divination to gather more information about the situation.

The Two of Air in a reading signifies clear guidance. All the necessary information is at hand and it is time to make a decision. The truth of the matter is clear, if only we open our eyes and accept it.

The shadow side of this card indicates that while the truth is indeed knowable, we are not ready or able to accept or deal with it at this time.

Three of Air: Scrying

Many forms of divination rely upon interpreting signs or symbols. The forms vary in the way that those signs and symbols are acquired. Scrying is done with anything with a reflective surface, although objects with a dark background are generally considered more effective, such as a dark bowl filled with water or a black mirror (a pane of glass painted black on the back, usually placed within a frame). Crystal balls are also common. A pond or any still (or nearly still) body of water can be used.

Scrying is simple. Sitting before your scrying tool, gaze at the surface softly, letting your eyes unfocus. Breathing slowly and steadily, enter a light meditative state. Let the images emerge from the depths of your scrying tool and reveal themselves on the surface.

Incorporating extra actions or attending to other considerations enhances some divination practices or considerations. As with dream work, burning the appropriate herbs aids in scrying. In addition, many practitioners prefer to cast a circle before beginning and to only scry during a new or full moon.

The Three of Air represents finding the truth by looking at something with different eyes or from another point of view. Just as a reflective scrying surface is different than a mirror and shows hidden yet significant information, so we find unperceived yet important truths when looking at something through a different lens.

The shadow side of this card indicates deception or misinformation caused by a distorted perception. The truth is hidden or obscured because we are seeing it through either a dark or perhaps a rose-colored lens.

As Above

Four of Air: Omens

Omens are a really interesting way for the Divine to communicate with us. Omens are simple things that occur in everyday life but somehow significant. Some are common omens, sometimes called superstitions, such as one we see in the card image of a black cat crossing someone's path. These types of omens are not always accepted or recognized by practicing witches.

We are more likely to pay attention to signals, animals, words, images, or situations that both happen a certain number of times in a short period of time or have intensely personal significance to the recipient. Most often omens are received unbidden. That is, we don't ask for an omen to occur. Usually, it is a way the Universe has of getting our attention and helping us know we are on the right path. Many think of this as synchronicity. For example, multiple sightings of a certain type of bird or animal can convey a message to the viewer. While dreams are seen as gifts from the Divine, omens can be considered as a friendly and helpful smack over the head with a baseball bat.

Utilizing omens does not take much effort on our part. We usually don't even need to be paying particular attention, as omens are often glaring and obviously unusual. However, the wise witch will always keep a watchful eye on her environment.

The Four of Air is a sign that the answer is right in front of our eyes. It is an affirmation by the Universe regarding a course of action or a situation.

The shadow side of this card indicates the Universe advising against a proposed plan or decision.

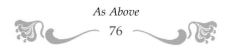

Five of Air: Palmistry

We have access to many keys to self-knowledge, and it is wise to make use of them, for as the ancient oracle once advised: Know thyself. We can look within ourselves and seek with truth of our hearts. We can look without and seek direction from the world around us. We can also look at ourselves, for we hold information within the very palms of our hands.

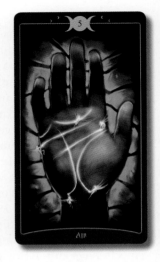

By learning to read our heart and head lines, we discover how we are naturally inclined to behave in relationships, most comfortable communicating, and likely to approach learning. Life and fate lines reveal information that can help us best understand and care for our physical bodies and to what extent we might be controlled by external circumstances. The shape of our palms provides clues about our character.

Reading your palm or having it read is not a once in a lifetime event for several reasons. First, the lines of your hand can change over time as you change. Second, even if the lines haven't changed, the way you may perceive or utilize the information may very well change. Reassessing both the information gathered and your reactions to it will help you better understand your own strengths and weaknesses.

The Five of Air says that it is important that our own strengths should be recognized and used to the best advantage at this time. We have what we need, but we may have to remind ourselves of that.

The shadow side of this card indicates that we are allowing circumstances to control us, that we are giving our power over to an assumed fate.

As Above

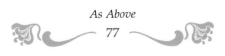

Six of Air: Familiar

Witches have a deep and special connection with nature, including animals. And, as with all nature, we have much to learn from our fellow creatures. Also, we recognize the existence of worlds other than the physical and are acquainted with beings that may not be considered "real" animals, but exist in some form nonetheless. There are many levels of relationships that we can have with animals, be they physical creatures or spiritual.

Animals take on the role of totem, spirit guide, power, and familiar. All of these aspects have differences and similarities and definitions vary among different spiritual paths and practices. Two things that they all have in common, though, are that we can learn from these animals and draw energy from them. Practitioners may form deep and lasting relationships with their power animals or spirit guides, or their paths may cross only for a short time.

Whether we call our special animal companion a guide or a familiar, whether we interact with them on the physical plane or on another plane, we turn to them for many things, including guidance, direction, moral support, companionship, strength, understanding, and healing.

The Six of Air points to relying on or deepening our connection with our animal helpers. In this case, their wisdom, guidance, or healing is needed. An animal guide will bring an important message.

The shadow side of this card indicates that there is an animal guide that we have not met yet or some external help that we are neglecting to listen to.

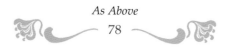

The Seven of Air: I Ching

The I Ching, also known as the Book of Changes, is an ancient Chinese text containing the divinatory meanings for each of the possible sixty-four hexagrams. Hexagrams are six stacked horizontal lines, which are determined (traditionally) by the tossing of yarrow sticks, although sometimes coins are used or even a random number generator. The outcome of the sticks or coins determines a line of the hexagram. A line is either solid or unbroken line (called Yang) or a broken or open line (called Yin). The sticks or coins are tossed a total of six times to create the hexagram that contains the message or answer for the seeker.

While the divinatory fortunes generated by the I Ching may certainly prove useful, what is more interesting to note is the concept of Yin and Yang. This concept, represented by the undoubtedly familiar Yin Yang symbol shown on the Seven of Air, explores how apparently contradictory forces or ideas contain within them the seed of their opposite. Although this is an oversimplification, Yang can be thought of as active or masculine and Yin as passive or feminine. But both are needed in order for each to exist or survive.

The Seven of Air reminds us that, just as Yin exists within Yang and Yang within Yin, so your answer lies within your question. Examine what you are asking and find the wisdom and guidance that dwells there.

The shadow side of this card indicates that the answer is not within the question because it is the wrong question. You should be asking something else.

Eight of Air: Meditation

Meditation is, arguably, one of the most useful skills a person, witch or not, can practice because it has so many uses. The most basic is to help calm the mind and focus on our connection with the Divine. Others include journeying, visualizing, and mental magic.

Meditation can be practiced many ways. But to start out, simply sit or lay flat in a way that is comfortable, on a chair, on the floor, on the bed, it doesn't matter as long as you won't be disturbed. Center your energy and ground yourself. Close your eyes, breath slowly for a few breaths, and quiet your mind. Be still and focus on your breath going in and coming out. Feel the calming, grounding energy of the earth fill you while nervous, anxious, or any unneeded energy flows back into the earth to be distributed as needed. Remain in this state for as long as you like, but most people begin with three to five minutes.

Instead of meditating with closed eyes, some people like to gaze at a candle or the smoke of a burning incense. This practice can also evolve into scrying. Beyond clearing and calming the mind, the opportunities presented by meditation are endless. By entering into deeper states, you can take journeys to different planes of existence, visit the spirit world, and meet your spirit guides. You can dialogue with aspects of the God or Goddess. To do any of these, set your intent before you begin.

You can do an important part of any magic: visualize. Clearly seeing your desired goal helps bring it into existence. You can perform mental magic by entering meditation and in your mind perform a spell, as an example, for protection. While in meditation, connect this spell with a small, unnoticeable movement, such as touching your thumb to your ring finger on your left hand (it can be any small movement). Then, while you are out and about your daily business and feel you need protection, just perform the movement you connected with the spell and instantly cast it. To do any of these, set your intent before you begin. Depending on what you wish to accomplish, you may wish to cast a circle. However, for short mind calming meditations, most people do find that necessary.

Meditation has many uses, but it has traditionally been used to quiet the mind and allow us to hear the quiet voice of wisdom deep within. The wisdom of the Divine is in all things, including us. We just need to be quiet enough to hear it.

The Eight of Air says to not underestimate the power of our mind. In this situation, the mind is the key. First, calm it; do not let it obsess. Second, focus it; decide the best way to employ its power. Finally, control it. Maintain connection to the Divine and keep it on task.

The shadow side of this card indicates that the mind has rather gone amok. While thoughts are allowed to run rampant and out of control, they create chaos and havoc.

Nine of Air: Runes

Runes are an alphabet, and there are several kinds of runes. However, here we refer to the runes given to Odin, the Norse god, who pierced his own side and hung for nine days on the World Tree without food or water, sacrificing himself so that he may gain wisdom and know the mysteries of the world.

Runes mince no words and do not suffer fools gladly. Blunt sometimes to the point of obscurity. The mysteries of the word can be found and learned and understood, but at a cost. Sacrifice is required. Knowledge or information or words, which especially in this age, can be had in great quantities for free. Wisdom, however, that must be earned.

In addition to using runes as a divinatory tool, runes are often used (and by some witches more often used) as a magical element. Using the runic alphabet, talismans can be created with very specific goals and powers. These can get very complex and precise by combining two or more runic letters. Selecting a rune that suits your purpose and carving into a small piece of wood or using a marker to mark it on a small stone are easy ways to create effective talismans.

The Nine of Air is a bittersweet card, for it promises great wisdom but the way to that wisdom includes suffering and sacrifice. Wisdom is not a right we are guaranteed. It is a reward, something earned. And it does not always promise happiness.

The shadow side of this card indicates that the situation contains aspects or information for which we are not prepared. It is best to walk past this path at this time and return to it later.

Ten of Air: Tarot

Tarot cards, like meditation, have so many uses. First, we of course use them to divine the way the future is trending, gauging the way the energy is flowing in terms of a situation, to catch a helpful glimpse of the future. Tarot works well for all sorts of topics, and can also be used in magic (with the Aces used, in a pinch, to represent the elements in a circle). The cards are used sometimes in meditation by selecting one that we feel holds a particular message that we need at the time, looking at the card until we can see it with our eyes closed, and then, after entering our meditative state, jour-

neying into the card and interacting with the characters and creatures that we find there.

Perhaps even more important is that the tarot not only tells us about possible futures, it can also give us guidance in creating alternate futures. If a particular reading presents a displeasing outcome, ask the tarot for advice to change the situation.

The cards of a tarot deck are like the unbound pages of a book. Whenever they are shuffled, new possibilities are created. They help us visualize the futures that we wish to create.

The Ten of Air indicates much power and control over the situation. Things are moving in a beneficial direction. And if they are not, be assured that you can easily change that.

The shadow side of this card indicates that in this case, the cards have been dealt and there is not much opportunity for getting fresh ones. You will have to play the hand that you were dealt with as much skill as possible.

As Above

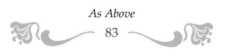

The Suit of Water

The Goddess and her many aspects play an important role in modern witchcraft. Perhaps because so many current practitioners had experience only in male-dominated religions, the feminine aspect of the Divine appeals to many. Of course, modern practitioners strive to many balance and recognize all forms of the Divine, there is no denying that many are drawn powerfully to the Goddess.

As we know, an important part of witchcraft is knowing, not just believing in, the Goddess. This knowing is based on experience, experience that is only gained by personal relationship with Her. While the Great Goddess herself may be largely unknowable due to our limitations of comprehension, She (as well as the Great God) shows herself in aspects, like facets of a diamond. We cannot always know Her in Her entirety, but we can know Her different faces. She and the Great God will meet us where we are.

The Suit of Water is particularly well-suited to an exploration of some of the Goddesses forms, as this suit focuses on relationships and particularly how our feelings and emotions shape our relationships and vice versa.

Suggested Reading List
The Goddess Guide by Priestess Brandi Auset
The Goddess Pages by Laurie Sue Brockway
Goddess Afoot by Michelle Skye
Goddess Alive by Michelle Skye
The Goddess Companion by Patricia Monaghan
Goddess Inspiration Oracle by Kris Waldherr
Universal Goddess Tarot by Maria Caratti and Antonella Platano

Ace of Water: The Chalice and the Athame

The Sabbats that we celebrate represent the turning of the Wheel of the year. Part of the Wheel is when the Maiden Goddess unites with the God. Through this union, she contains the seed of the year to come, insuring that all life will continue on earth. Witches sometimes commemorate this event with a symbolic ceremony called the Great Rite. The Great Rite takes one of two forms. In one, the High Priestess and the High Priest of a coven perform a ritual together in which they embody the Goddess and the God, culminating in intercourse, symbolizing the Sacred Marriage. Another, perhaps more common ritual, is to symbolize the Sacred Marriage using a Chalice filled with wine to represent the Goddess and an athame to represent the God.

The Ace of Water represents a relationship that promises to grow into something more – something fulfilling, something powerful, something divine.

The shadow side of this card indicates discounting a relationship before giving it time to blossom.

Two of Water: Love

It seems that so many of the various pan-
theons have complicated stories and relationships, but none more so than the
Greek and Roman divinities. And, as we
know, love and romantic relationships
are extremely complex. So it is fitting
that Aphrodite and Eros (or Venus and
Cupid, if you prefer the Roman names)
adorn this card, representing love.

Interestingly, Aphrodite is also associated
with wars and illicit affairs, both of which
seem to occur when love goes wrong.

Aphrodite is not a simpering goddess
who fawns over any male she wishes to attract. Instead, she is completely herself. She values and cares for herself. Her strength and
confidence are compelling and attractive.

The Two of Water promises a romantic, loving relationship. The
two people involved will be quite enthralled with each other. Being so wrapped up in their own little world, they may neglect other things for a while.

The shadow side of this card indicates the possibility of love going wrong. The first blush of love or the honeymoon phase may
be over.

Three of Water: Creation/Fertility

The Roman goddess Flora is known for her association with springtime and the flowering of the plants. She protects plants from rotting and helps young girls as they approach womanhood. Everything about her is young and fresh and filled with beauty and promises for the future.

Within her creation, the fragrant blossoms of spring, are many blessings. The color and scents revive and refresh our spirits after months of winter dreariness. Within the flowers are elements that will eventually become fruits and vegetables, to nourish our bodies throughout the year. Of course, there is also the promise the death and decay, as part of the natural cycle of life, but for now, all is lovely, lush, and delightful.

The Three of Water denotes a happy time of plenty. There is not just enough but more than enough; enough to put by for a rainy day. Having something set aside gives a sense of security that makes the present even more enjoyable.

The shadow side of this card indicates a lack or a lack of appreciation for what is available.

Four of Water: Healing

Brigid is a popular goddess and associated with many things. In fact, we've already met her in this deck, in arcana XVII, Imbolc. Here, the symbols, such as the apple tree and the caduceus are used to point to her role as healer. She, among other things, the keeper of the holy wells and rivers that flow with healing waters.

She also holds up a flame, for while most healing is soothing and cooling like the waters of her well some healing requires more aggressive actions. Sometimes things must not just be washed away, but utterly destroyed in order achieve a full healing. The application of pain may be necessary in order to alleviate pain.

The Four of Water brings with it the promise of healing of some sort – emotional, physical, or perhaps of a relationship. Although there may be a bit of pain involved, the long run promises relief and smooth sailing.

The shadow side of this card indicates ignoring a situation that needs attention. The situation needs to be attended to or the resulting festering could cause irreparable damage.

Five of Water: War
Older even than the classical Roman pantheon, Bellona is an Etruscan goddess of
war. As we noticed with Aphrodite, war
is sometimes closely linked with love and
relationships. We don't mean war in the
usual sense, of course. In terms of relationships, the word "war" is symbolic
for a clashing of wills and desires, when
one party wants something that the other
party does not want.

Bellona, as a war goddess, is particularly invoked for victory and for something
that is very useful in obtaining that victory: strategy. While Bellona may wield
common elements of physical destruction...swords and spears...
one assumes her most deadly weapon is her mind. The reminder
here is to make sure your strategy is sound before taking your first
step. Be clear on what you want to achieve and think through the
very best way to achieve it. It may be difficult, for as the belladon-
na symbolizes, danger and deception are all around.

The Five of Water indicates a highly dramatic situation with all
parties involved feeling highly charged and restless. Communication is off. Relationships are faltering. It will take a cool head to
navigate this situation.

The shadow side of this card indicates chaos and wanton destruction – physical, emotional, or relationships. Things are being said
or done that will bring about no good to anyone.

Six of Water: Wisdom and Culture

Sarasvati is a Hindu goddess who gave people language, science, math, the arts – including music, dancing, and poetry. She created learning and teaching. She gave us ways to understand our world and our selves as well as the means to creatively express how we feel and what we think about all that we learn and see and experience.

Relationships of all sorts, emotions, affairs and questions and longings of the heart – these are all common inspiration for artistic expression. Through the gifts of Sarasvati, we can better understand and articulate our uniquely human experiences. While not all of what we learn or experience is pleasant, through art we can find ways to use those experiences to both create beauty and to communicate and connect with our fellow travelers on this journey through life.

The Six of Water speaks of creative expression of feelings and thoughts in a way that helps you understand yourself better or that allows you to develop a deeper connection another person or other people. Channel your feelings creatively.

The shadow side of this card indicates a lack of appreciation for finer things or refusing to understand or connect with one who is trying to establish common ground.

Seven of Water: Justice

Ma'at is the Egyptian goddess of justice, divine order, truth, and moral law. Her job is to weigh the heart of the departed against her feather of truth. If she is satisfied with the accounting, the soul moves on. If not, the soul is destroyed. Ma'at's final decisions and power are such that even the other gods and goddesses must abide by her determination.

Ma'at represents the rules of order that keep the universe moving forward and not falling into chaos. A strict balance must be observed, and very likely the ancient Egyptians no doubt had their own ideas about how this all worked. However, Ma'at does not represent just the Egyptian worldview. For us, today, she can represent our own views of justice and truth and balance. She is a symbol for what we believe is the ideal heart, the one that lives most closely aligned with our beliefs of what is right.

The Seven of Water is a time of accounting. It is time to consider our actions and measure them against our beliefs. We should be living according to what we claim to be right. Before acting, we ask ourselves: is this the action of the person I wish to be?

The shadow side of this card indicates that we are not living according to our beliefs and that we will, at some point, be required to pay more than we'd like for the luxury of this decision.

Eight of Water:
Magic and Transformation

Cerridwen is a popular Welsh goddess and is associated with many things: prophecy, magic, death, rebirth, divine wisdom, and inspiration. In this instance, we are thinking about her as the goddess of the cauldron. A cauldron is symbolic of a place where magic happens… that is, where something is transformed into something else. Cerridwen is, perhaps, best known as the goddess of the cauldron. For it is said in some versions of the myth that it was in a cauldron that she created Taliesan, the famous bard, although in some versions, her womb symbolized the cauldron.

Magically speaking, whenever we cast a circle, we create a type of cauldron, a place of out place and a time out of time, a safe place where magic occurs.

The Eight of Water is a time of powerful change. Your intent and decisions will have long term ramifications and will shape the directions being determined at this time. You have the power to create the transformation that you seek.

The shadow side of this card indicates stagnation. The power is available but is not being utilized at all, or is not being used in the most beneficial manner.

Nine of Water: Prosperity

Lakshmi is the beloved Hindu goddess of prosperity. She governs over abundance and wealth, both material and spiritual. She is known for her generosity, freely giving to all those who would but receive her gifts. No matter how much she shares, she never runs short, for there is more than enough for everyone. There is no moral judgment about which sort of prosperity – material or spiritual – is more desirable. Lakshmi and her devotees love and honor both, for one is the reflection of the other: another instance of "as above, so below."

An interesting law seems to be at work with Lakshmi – it seems that she is able to give without restriction and by doing so only increases her own prosperity and her generosity. In a symbiotic twist, she needs those to give to in order to increase her own blessings. Likewise, it would seem that we also, in order to fully enjoy our blessings, need others with whom to share. Lakshmi seems to teach us that giving increases rather than lessens our prosperity.

The Nine of Water promises increased prosperity, both material and spiritual, as well as others to share it with. Blessings and gifts and revelations abound as if from nowhere, simple in response to your own generous actions and simple requests.

The shadow side of this card indicates the presence of prosperity coupled with the inability to receive or accept the blessings. Turning your back on gifts.

Ten of Water: The Otherworld

Hecate is a triple-faced Greek goddess with power over heaven, earth, and the underworld. As with most goddesses, she has many associations. Here she is shown in her role as Queen of the Ghosts. She protects ghosts from harm and also keeps them from doing mischief in our world. Hecate is often found at crossroads and at borders and boundaries. She is at home in liminal places. She navigates the space just between places, where things are shady and where it is easy to get lost.

In our lives or in our relationships, there are spaces such as these, gray and uncertain. In these spaces, we can call on Hecate, who knows how to see and how to communicate with those who dwell on both sides of the line. For us, the Otherworld can mean the place where spirits dwell or it can symbolize those we are separated from and to whom we cannot seem to find our way back.

The Ten of Water brings you squarely to a place of uncertainty and forces you to do something. There are people who you need to find or spirits you need to contact. Allowing the fog and haze to grow between you and whoever is no longer an option.

The shadow side of this card indicates that you are wandering in the mists starting at shadows and are obsessed with finding something or someone who is not there.

The Suit of Earth

Most religions and spiritual paths have sacred texts, such as the Bible or the Koran. For us having no single holy book to share and to build upon, we turn to our God and our Goddess. We trace the movement of the Sun and Moon through the sky and watch the stars twinkle in the heavens. Across thousands of miles, these heaven-bound bodies teach, comfort, and inspire. However, we have a more intimate connection as well. The Earth – our home and our mother – is our most sacred of texts.

From the Earth we not only have a home and knowledge, but also power. Everything that exists on the Earth has its own energy and magic and power – crystals, stones, trees, plants, bodies of water, animals, insects, simply everything. We can learn about it and interact with it until we know enough to use it effectively, to be comfortable with the flow. The Earth – our symbol for stability, and yet it is ever-moving, beneath its surface and through space, and everything upon it and in its waters moves.

Suggested Reading List
Field Guide to the Little People by Nancy Arrowsmith
Plant Spirit Journey by Laura Silvana
Follow the Shaman's Call by Mike Williams
Connecting to the Power of Nature by Joe H. Slate
Crystal Awareness by Catherine Bowman
Crystals for Beginners by Corrine Kenner
Essential Herbal Wisdom by Nancy Arrowsmith
Inner Journeys by Gloria Chawick
Mother Nature's Herbal by Judith Griffin
Flower and Tree Magic by Richard Webster
Herb Magic for Beginners by Ellen Dugan
Earth Power by Scott Cunningham

Ace of Earth: The Human Body

Making the Ace the human body does not mean that humans are first priority or the center of the universe, although sometimes we act like that. Rather, it represents that our experience of the world starts with our body. We perceive through our physical senses as well as with our heart and our mind, our instincts and intuition. Everything that exists must be known, because we cannot do so otherwise, through our own unique experience. And what we bring to the that experience, like an observer watching subatomic particles, effects and shapes what is learned. We cannot separate ourselves from environment no matter how much we behave to the contrary.

The Ace of Earth contains the potential one could hope for. Everything that exists or can exist is in this Ace. It is the seed of Universe. When this card shows up, it is a gift, a sign that you can make a lot with very little.

The shadow side of this card indicates squandering a gift or refusing to see its value and potential.

Two of Earth: Beach

The beach, where earth meets ocean, where stable land gives way to shifting sand, leading out to water and an alien-like world. Like the places that Hecate rules, the beach is a liminal place, a portal from one world to another. The space is not always clearly defined, either. The tides move in and out, changing the boundaries and creating new, temporary environments. Tidal pools are filled with mysteries and treasures. There is a sense of entering an exotic world filled with beauty and dangers that we know little about.

The Two of Earth is a balance: water and earth. They live here as equals. The earth does not contain the water entirely, and the water does not destroy the earth. Our physical experience and our soul can balance and nurture and enhance each other, and in fact that is what this card calls for.

The shadow side of this card indicates that the body and soul are out of balance or disconnected. Extreme habits or practices are causing determent to not only itself, but the other as well.

Three of Earth: Plant life

The life cycle of plants is one of our most common metaphors. We speak often of seeds and soil and watering and weeding. We speak of birds and bees. We observe the Wheel of the Year and it is impossible to not think immediately of where plants are in their cycle. Plants are part of the earth, and also of the sun and of water and of air. And they, these marvelous works of art and scientific wonder and the four elements, are our food. We are nourished with such miracles. And plants are often an important part of our magical work. They contain and release energy, chemicals, and qualities that are easy for us to access and understand. They are excellent partners. Through the plants, we learn a different aspect of earth, for the plants are more fragile and usually have a shorter life span than more earthy symbols of earth, such as rocks. But then, plants are alive in a way that rocks are not. It is a trade off.

The Three of Earth is the result of what can be done when different elements combine together. Working with others or as part of team will allow you to accomplish more or even something entirely different than if you were to work alone.

The shadow side of this card indicates that a group or team is not working together very well. Their end result will likely not be all that was hoped for.

Four of Earth: Stones and crystals

Stones and rocks, whether small enough to fit comfortably in the palm of our hands or huge boulders that we wouldn't dream of trying to move, are one of the most quintessential symbols of the Earth. The have a sense of stability, of being grounded, of endurance, of time – of having been here forever and being here forever. Like herbs and plants, stones and crystals all have their own natures and characteristics. We can learn about them and find ways to work with them. It is like the Earth hides pieces of Herself, Her magic, and Her power away in stones and crystals and leaves them scattered for us to find. We can gather and collect these gifts, saving them until needed.

The Four of Earth is power, resources, and energy that have been collected and stored, put in a safe place until needed. This is a time to store, to save, to conserve. There will come a time when all that you've saved will come in handy.

The shadow side of this card indicates that resources, energy, or power are being squandered. Spending or using your stores now is not a wise investment.

Five of Earth: Mountains and waterfall

Mountains are formed by intense power – they are thrust upwards by the meeting of continental plates, formed by molten metal and stone erupting from deep within the earth, or by huge glaciers carving and depositing great quantities of earth as they move. Looking at them, though, we are struck by majesty, sheer size, and a sense of immobility. Water, usually a passive, softly flowing element, gains momentum and strength as it passes over a mountain and falls back down to earth. It in fact, can become as powerful and destructive as a falling boulder. The very water that gains its strength from the mountain slowly erodes the mountain, wearing it down ever so slowly. Eventually, the water will win this long battle.

The Five of Earth illustrates lengthy scenarios. Whatever is going on will not resolve quickly. The situation started much earlier than you may think and will continue longer. There are ways to gain strength and eventually achieve your goals through patient consistency.

The shadow side of this card indicates that you are giving up too soon or are becoming too distracted. Instead of constant steps forward, you are taking one step forward and then two steps back.

Six of Earth: Trees and forest

Trees, both singly and grouped together, are fraught with meaning for us. In Celtic tree lore, specific trees have very definite meanings. Trees are used in journeying, as a starting place from which to access the underworld, the upperworld, and the otherworld. The life cycle of trees are a visible reminder of the Wheel of the Year while evergreens are a constant reminder to have hope and faith.

Groups of trees can provide both places of safety and respite as well as places of danger and fear. The forest is the home of many creatures and we humans are not always comfortable in the woods. It is often dark and because we cannot see the horizon or even very far at all nor the sun, it is easy to feel lost and confused. However, in such a dark, confused mess, it is easier to see your path, should you be lucky enough to stumble upon it.

The Six of Earth represents moving from one place to another. This is something that helps you transition from one state to another state. It provides a touchstone that you can always return to when needed. It is a safe place that protects and also prepares you for what is to come.

The shadow side of this card indicates a dark and confused situation filled with unknown elements. They may likely be dangerous...and may just as likely not be dangerous. But, really, at this point, there is no way to know.

Seven of Earth: Sea creatures

Creatures of the sea seem so very different from us who dwell on the land and breathe air. However, it is interesting to remember that for nine months or so, each of us breathed liquid. It was our first experience in breathing and once born, we were somewhat shocked into breathing air.

Despite our shared breathing experience, living under the water is still different than living on the earth. The difference, really, is water versus air. It seems that it would be easier to feel the flow of the universe in water, that one could sense upcoming eddies and currents and learn to work with them to move effectively and efficiently through life. The creatures of the sea seem to do this. Perhaps we, if we practiced being more sensitive, could also learn to sense the movement of our environment and of the universe around us.

The Seven of Earth indicates that now is a time to move carefully, to pay attention to your environment, to be extra sensitive to energetic flow. Move and experience things differently than normal. Recognize that this is a new situation and adjust your perceptions accordingly. Flow as gracefully as possible, without jarring or upsetting the balance.

The shadow side of this card indicates being in a new situation and feeling uncomfortable. You are having trouble acclimating and are uncertain how to react and behave. Your struggles will wear you out and probably make things worse.

Eight of Earth: Air creatures
Like trees, we imbue creatures of the air with so many symbolic meanings, both specifically and generally. As a group, they are associated with the element of air, of course, and therefore with thoughts and communications, particularly we think of them as messengers from the God and Goddess. With their ability to fly, we cannot help but thing of freedom. Specifically, crows and ravens are associated with the Goddess. Butterflies bring to mind transformation. Bees represent love, productivity, and the possibility of the impossible. With our sea creature brethren, we tend to think of where we came from. The creatures flitting through the air make our souls and mind sing with ideas of what we might become.

The Eight of Earth asks you to reach higher, stretch farther, and dream bigger. Whatever it is you are attempting, it is not even close to what is potentially possible. Slough off whatever baggage is holding you earthbound. Make yourself as light as possible by letting go of doubts and focusing on what you know is possible.

The shadow side of this card indicates that the Universe is communicating with you, but you are not hearing it or are misinterpreting it. There is a danger that you'll assume more than is possible, and like Icarus, attempt too much.

Nine of Earth: Land creatures

As we peer into the depths of the seas, we look upon our past. When we lift our eyes to the skies, we imagine the future. In the middle, firmly between past and future, is the present, right where it always is. Here, in the present, we do what needs doing. While there are many, many animals that walk the earth with us, this cow, standing solidly in her field, contentedly munching her grass, is the epitome of being present. She is not concerned about what will happen later or fretting about something she forgot to do earlier. Instead, she smells the freshness of the air, feels the cool breeze, and enjoys the  taste of sweet grass. It is a state that is both sensual and spiritual, knowing that one is exactly where one should be and is enjoying it to the fullest.

The Nine of Earth points to a time of satisfaction and satiation. There is enough of everything…and it is all very enjoyable. Like a perfect summer evening or sunny spring afternoon, all is just right. The wisest thing to do is nothing.

The shadow side of this card indicates a pre-occupation with the past or the future. Frantically fretting and worrying will not only not solve anything, but will in this case cause something important to be overlooked.

Ten of Earth: A full day

As we've noted before, the world seems solid and firm to us, but it is really moving quite quickly in a number of different ways all at once. Probably the most notable one is the Earth's rotation on its axis, causing the experience of day and night. The division of our time on this planet into lightness and darkness is also one of our most persistent and common metaphors: yin/yang. Everything carries the seed of its opposite. The night sky has the moon, which reflects the sun, the orb of the day. The day casts shadows, seeds of night under the sun. And yet there is a sense of eternity, for the stars shine always, whether we see them or not.

The combination of opposites reminds us that there is a time for everything. Work, play, sleep. Activity and rest. Planting and sowing. Giving and receiving. Sometimes we play one role, sometimes another. But always and eternally, whether we notice or not, the God and the Goddess shine and flow through it all.

The Ten of Earth denotes a special awareness of the balance of time. There is an appropriate time and place for what you want to do. Right now you are able to tap into the universal flow and know exactly when that time is. Honor what you know to be true and practice patience, as you may be tempted to move ahead of time.

The shadow side of this card indicates that now is clearly not the right time. You are not in a position to judge the proper time at the moment. Wait things out a bit before acting.

As Above

SO BELOW

So Below is a more traditional tarot deck than the *As Above* Tarot. Whereas *As Above* has been restructured in order to teach some of the main points of paganism, *So Below* follows what many tarot readers call the RWS tradition. Anyone familiar with a RWS pack will easily be able to read with this deck. However, anyone who is a pagan or magical practitioner will find this deck more relevant than the RWS tarot and more deeply resonant. It really can play two roles. It works with *As Above* to complete the analogy of the Hermetic Principle "As Above, So Below," giving the user a deeper and broader tarot reading experience. It also is traditional enough to work as a daily or common reading deck. The vibrant art makes it an ideal choice when doing several readings back to back or in a lively location.

In many ways, this deck can be read like an ordinary RWS-style deck. But there is a little more here that can add power to your readings. In all of the images, we see Elemental Energy experienced, utilized, or even ignored. Noting this can add depth to your readings, as you can get ideas for how to magically influence the situation in question or understand how you are using your own energy or power against yourself. Sometimes when the human characters are not consciously utilizing magic, the energy present is still represented and can be channeled within the context of the situation being explored in the reading.

Because this deck is designed to echo traditional decks and indeed to be used in the same way, reversed meanings are given for all the cards. Reversals are a very personal decision. Feel free to not use them at all or to use your own methods for interpreting them.

The Major Arcana

As with most tarot decks, here the Major cards represent big events in our lives, situations or forces beyond our control, and decisions or experiences with karmic implications. These cards also reflect the human experience of the *As Above* Major Arcana cards.

0, The Fool

The Fool lets her magic flow, trusting in the universe and allowing serendipity to control everything. She has no plan or agenda except for enjoying the day. Her trust is touching and sweet and it is, perhaps, why she is so in touch with her intuition, which provides her a measure of protection.

Divinatory meaning: Carefree, trusting the universe, following your intuition.
Reversed: Making foolish or poor choices. Not listening to reason.

I, The Magician

The Magician has all her tools in place, has created her sacred space, and is clear on what she hopes to accomplish. She is but a few short moments and a few important words away from manifesting change in her life and in the world.

Divinatory meaning: Using knowledge, resources, and will to create positive change in the world.
Reversed: Using abilities for negative purposes or manipulating others.

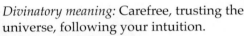

II, The High Priestess

The High Priestess is the keeper of dark, mysterious knowledge. Because what she gives cannot be taught or explained logically, it sometimes seems scary. But there is no way around it. It must be experienced to be known. Muster up some trust, take her hand, and dive in.

Divinatory meaning: Connection with the Divine, a deep and certain knowledge.
Reversed: Confusing emotional reaction with spiritual certainty.

III, The Empress

The Empress expresses herself beautifully in the physical world. She helps things grow by making them comfortable, by feeding them what they need to become strong, and by healing injuries. She loves and comforts and blesses all that come within her realm.

Divinatory meaning: Abundance, nurturing, and creation.
Reversed: Smothering or controlling someone or something in the name of love.

IV, The Emperor

The Emperor is the one everyone wants to be in charge. No matter if the group is planning a party, a fundraiser, or a political event, the right leader makes all the different. The Emperor will organize and delegate, making sure that resources and skills are employed in the most efficient possible way.

Divinatory meaning: Creating order and stability, planning, and organizing for the greater good.
Reversed: Valuing rigidity and order for their own sake.

V, The Hierophant/The Teacher

The Teacher understands the theory behind things. She also knows that moving from theory to practical application is not always a smooth translation. She helps other understand not only the whys and wherefores of a subject, but she also helps them apply knowledge to their everyday lives in ways that make for them.

Divinatory meaning: Making knowledge accessible and understandable to others.
Reversed: Using knowledge as a way to control or wield power.

VI, The Lovers

The Lovers are two people (or sometimes a single person, for this card is not always about romantic relationships) who commit to a certain path, who decide to pursue a certain long-term goal. This is not some random or spontaneous decision. They are in it for the duration and intend to see it to the very end. Consequently, it should be a well-considered decision that includes much soul-searching as well as a good balance between the heart and mind.

Divinatory meaning: Making decisions that honor the wisdom of the heart.
Reversed: Doing something for the wrong reasons.

VII, The Chariot

The Chariot either has a lot going on or is focused on one large task. The only way she will succeed is to focus, focus, focus. There is no room for distractions or daydreams. Single-minded determination is the key.

Divinatory meaning: The triumph of will in difficult circumstances; the ability to do what needs to be done.
Reversed: Losing control; a situation that got out of hand; chaos.

VIII, Strength

Strength knows her potential is vast. She knows that she actually cannot comprehend the extent of her own ability. But she also realizes all of that Divine potential is encased in a human body. And so Strength knows when to push and when to ease back. The testing of limits is necessary but it is during rest that strength is achieved.

Divinatory meaning: The elegant mastery of self.
Reversed: Heavy-handed control in the name of discipline; repressed desires.

IX, The Hermit

The Hermit knows that she must sometimes put herself first. Downtime has to be a priority. Without it, she cannot recharge her soul. As she continues to grow and change she must continually reassess her beliefs. Retreating from distractions to touch base with her own heart is not a once in a lifetime event, but a regular date with herself.

Divinatory meaning: Retreating from distractions to determine your own truth.
Reversed: Withdrawing from society to lick wounds or hide.

X, The Wheel of Fortune

The Wheel knows that she is continually in motion. The external expression of her experience is always changing. At the center, in the depths of her heart, she finds enough stability to not be upset or alarmed by the natural changes in life.

Divinatory meaning: The natural changes in life.
Reversed: Stagnation.

XI, Justice

Contrary to what some may think, Justice does not imply judgment but simple cause and effect. Everything that happens, happens for a reason. That reason is usually a past action on our part. Only we can determine if the price paid was a bargain or a bad deal.

Divinatory meaning: The consequences of your actions are at hand.
Reversed: Unfair or unwarranted results.

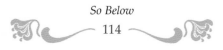

XII, The Hanged Man

The Hanged Man's situation is the opposite of The Chariot's. The only way through her situation is to let go, relax, accept, and learn. She cannot power through it. She cannot control it. Patient waiting is usually rewarded. When the time is right, then things can move forward.

Divinatory meaning: Willing surrender to an experience or situation.
Reversed: Unnecessary sacrifice; martyrdom.

XIII, Death

When something ends, there is a time of mourning. The difficult emotions – anger, bitterness, sadness, despair – are never enjoyable. They must be experienced, though. And within even these feelings are hidden gifts that deepen our character, enhance our compassion, and usher in new experiences.

Divinatory meaning: An ending of something important.
Reversed: Holding onto something that is over.

XIV, Temperance

Getting the perfect balance in anything creates an alchemy that yields magical results. It is not always easy and sometimes not enjoyable...until the end result is visible. Then you'll be very glad you did it right.

Divinatory meaning: Moderation and control; the right thing at the right time in the right place.
Reversed: Wildly erratic behavior.

XV, The Devil

Not matter how pretty or appealing a thing is, if it controls your will, it is not worth it. Everything is relative, so even something normally "positive" may not be in your best interest if it is the wrong time or the wrong amount or for the wrong reason.

Divinatory meaning: A choice, action, or situation contrary to your best interest.
Reversed: Mistakenly judging something as bad, negative, or wrong.

XVI, The Tower

Like lightning striking, unexpected changes seem to come out of nowhere, with no warning. In their wake, they leave the world altered forever and looking like quite a mess.

Divinatory meaning: An unexpected event that changes everything.
Reversed: Trying to avoid something by denial or delay leading to increased turmoil.

XVII, The Star

The Star is like pushing the reset button. It helps you feel clean, refreshed, and renewed. Cynicism and pessimism fall away and you can look at the world through new eyes, expecting good things.

Divinatory meaning: A time of renewal and cleansing.
Reversed: False hopes.

XVIII, The Moon

The Moon is beguiling and magical. It can reveal amazing mysterious. However, wandering around in the moonlight in an unknown environment is dangerous, as its light conceals more than it reveals. In such a landscape, it is easy for the mind to see monsters and fears where they may not exist.

Divinatory meaning: An uncertain situation both fraught with deception while revealing important truths.
Reversed: Being purposefully deceived.

XIX, The Sun

The Sun warms the earth, encouraging life and growth, fruit and flowers, adding sweetness to life. It punctuates the cycles of life. In its light, we celebrate all the things that we hold most dear.

Divinatory meaning: Connections, generations, and cycles that bring joy.
Reversed: Too many positive activities; feeling burnt out; need to prioritize.

XX, Judgement

If we ask, the Divine will answer. The key, though, is not only asking but also listening. After posing the question, keep your spirit calm enough to hear the response. Actively seek it, look forward to its arrival. And, by all means, prepare to act on it, for it will undoubtedly change your life.

Divinatory meaning: Receiving and hearing a spiritual message.
Reversed: Ignoring signs from the Divine. Being afraid of doing what's right.

XXI, The World

The World is much like The Fool, but with one important difference. She knows what she can do and what she should do. While she trusts in the Divine and in her intuition, she is more of an active partner with the Universe, helping co-create reality.

Divinatory meaning: Walking through life with confidence and creating harmony and magic with every step.
Reversed: Feeling more certain but not quite ready to step out into the world yet.

The As Above, So Below Major Arcanas

Earlier we mentioned how the two decks in this set reflect each other as two halves of an hourglass. The two Major Arcana decks overlap to form the funnel through which the energy of the Universe flow from the realms of the Divine into our daily lives…truly illustrating the Hermetic principle of "**as above, so below.**" As we compare the corresponding cards from both decks, we can see how the archetypal energy flows from one realm to the other. By making a study of these cards as pairs, we can learn about the card and how it exists as an archetype and how it exists as a facet of our reality. We can also better understand the nature of the energy of the card and how to work with it better, rather than against it.

The Fool
As Above: Creating the next lifetime
So Below: Creating the next moment

The Magician
As Above: The elements
So Below: Working with the elements

The High Priestess
As Above: Divine wisdom
So Below: Seeking and receiving wisdom

The Empress
As Above: The Great Goddess and the life cycle
So Below: Growing, nurturing, and healing

The Emperor
As Above: The Great God and the life cycle
So Below: Keeping the cycle moving

The Hierophant
As Above: Your sacred beliefs
So Below: Living those beliefs by teaching others

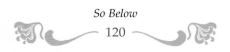

The Lovers
As Above: The Great Union that begins the life cycle
So Below: A choice that begins an important cycle

The Chariot
As Above: The Universe consciously transforming itself
So Below: The use of will to change a situation

Strength
As Above: Creating change on the spiritual plane
So Below: Creating change in the physical world

The Hermit
As Above: A spiritual journey to find truth
So Below: Retreating from the world to seek truth

The Wheel
As Above: The life cycles of the world
So Below: The life cycles of a person

Justice
As Above: Spiritual consequences
So Below: Consequences of daily actions

The Hanged Man
As Above: Creating sacred space for spiritual work
So Below: Finding inner sacred space

Death
As Above: The darkness that heralds the light
So Below: An ending that yields to a beginning

Temperance
As Above: Divine grace and inner balance
So Below: A balanced life

The Devil
As Above: Abandoning the spiritual for the physical
So Below: Overindulgence

The Tower
As Above: Divine warnings
So Below: Shocking news

The Star
As Above: Spiritual healing and hope
So Below: Refreshment and renewal

The Moon
As Above: The world of the Crone and the Dark Lord
So Below: Personal darkness and inner fears

The Sun
As Above: The zenith of Universal Energy
So Below: Personal success

Judgement
As Above: A spiritual calling
So Below: Seeking and receiving Divine communication

The World
As Above: The wholeness of the Divine
So Below: Feeling as one with the Universe

Minor Arcana

The Minor cards in a deck may be less impressive than the Major cards, but they have several important jobs to do in a reading. First, they represent the events of our everyday lives. Second, all the cards belong to one of four suits. Each suit has an elemental correspondence, so we can see at a glance what kind of energy is involved in or influencing the situation in question. Even though these cards differ from the As Above Tarot, the suits carry the same energy. Third, if there is more than one of any number in a reading, that gives additional information. For example, Aces indicate a gift or opportunity. Twos point out choices or decisions that need to be made. Fours represent stability or stagnation. Fives are a sign

of instability. Tens let you know a situation is nearing an end or resolution. The Minor Arcana are definitely like the worker bees of a tarot deck.

Ace of Cups

A gift of Divine love is offered. If it is accepted, the loving energy flows through the recipient, enhancing her life.

Divinatory meaning: An opportunity for an emotional experience or growth.

Reversed: A new relationship does not live up to its potential.

Two of Cups

These two souls recognize a connection and the space between them fairly radiates with positive energy. Like attracts like and so this draws the possibility of love or other deep relationship.

Divinatory meaning: Deep emotional connection or attraction.

Reversed: A lack of or a one-sided connection.

Three of Cups

These three women are gathered in a joyous celebration. The Divine blesses them and undines join the party. Their act creates more joy and brings happy energy into being.

Divinatory meaning: A spontaneous, unexpected joy or pleasure.

Reversed: An event or plans did not live up to your expectations.

Four of Cups

Three wonderful gifts are presented to this woman, but she does not care for any of them. Instead, she visualizes a fourth option. This situation could lead to manifesting something amazing or giving into depression. Which will she choose?

Divinatory meaning: Dissatisfaction with reality.

Reversed: Wallowing in ennui or self-pity.

Five of Cups

Things did not work out as this woman had hoped. Her expectations were not realized. Unfortunately, this does happen in life from time to time. Mourning is like calling to the Divine. It can come to comfort and heal.

Divinatory meaning: Reactions to loss and grief.

Reversed: Repression of grief.

Six of Cups

These people are totally in the moment. They are not aware of it yet, but they are creating a memory, a snapshot of their hearts, that will bring them happiness and perhaps even comfort in the future.

Divinatory meaning: Creating or thinking about happy memories.

Reversed: Romanticizing the past.

Seven of Cups:

The world is full of opportunities and we are full of potential, as this young woman now knows. The imagination is a great gift, for through it we can experience all possible futures and thereby commit to one and manifest it in our lives.

Divinatory meaning: Dreams and desires.

Reversed: Confusion and immobility.

Eight of Cups

No matter how carefully we choose our path and select a project to pursue, sometimes we make mistakes. When we realize we'd made a bad decision (or a good decision that no longer serves our highest good), then we, like this woman, should let it go and begin anew.

Divinatory meaning: Leaving something behind to start something else.

Reversed: Clinging to something that is no longer useful.

So Below

Nine of Cups

One of the first acts of magic every child learns is to "make a wish" when they blow out their birthday candles. This birthday girl seems to already have her wish, based on the happy and heartfelt companions around her.

Divinatory meaning: Material, emotional, and physical well being; the traditional "wish" card.

Reversed: Having plenty but wanting more; greed.

Ten of Cups

Tens are cards of completion as well as heralding a new cycle. An emotional attachment has begun and blossomed into a deeper commitment. This couple is celebrating the beginning of a new phase in their relationship based on the fullness of their hearts.

Divinatory meaning: A happy home life.

Reversed: Presenting a false face of domestic happiness to the world.

Ace of Pentacles

The gifts of the earth are laid before. When we choose to work with them, in harmony, they assist us in our endeavors. Any option pursued seems to carry unlimited potential.

Divinatory meaning: An opportunity for prosperity.

Reversed: An opportunity is not as lucrative as it appears.

Two of Pentacles

By attuning to the Elemental Energies, we, like this skilled woman, can work with the flow, balancing many tasks with grace and ending up with lovely creations.

Divinatory meaning: Maintaining balance, creating good things.

Reversed: Stressed; too much to do; unable to give anything its proper attention.

Three of Pentacles

After a flurry of activity and perhaps a little (or a lot) of mess, this woman's hard woman and passionate vision have paid off. She has created what she intended and seems very pleased with the result.

Divinatory meaning: Manifesting a goal.

Reversed: Stuck in the middle of a process; unable to finish something.

Four of Pentacles

The Wheel of the Year teaches us that there is a time to relax and enjoy the bounty of nature. Then, as the dark and cold days approach, we are wise to prepare for them. This woman will enjoy a reminder of the balmy days of summer when she opens one of her jars.

Divinatory meaning: Gathering power or resources.

Reversed: Hoarding resources; operating from a place of fear.

Five of Pentacles

Staying attuned to the flow of the Universe and the guidance of the Divine is not always easy. We get distracted. Then we feel lost. If we panic, we may miss the quiet signs that the Divine lovingly provides to help us get on back on the right path.

Divinatory meaning: Feeling lost and in need of resources and guidance.

Reversed: Ignoring help that offered.

Six of Pentacles

It seems that nobody ever has everything they want, so deciding how to use the resources you have is important. Decisions are not always clear and Divine guidance may feel absent. Trust the Universe and make your decision.

Divinatory meaning: Sharing material resources, prioritizing needs and wants.

Reversed: Not having enough to do everything you want.

Seven of Pentacles

After a season of work, it's natural to take a step back and analyze the situation. What worked, what didn't, what would you do differently? Apparently this women has concluded that her work in her orchard has paid off rather handsomely.

Divinatory meaning: Appraising results of efforts and finding them good.

Reversed: Dissatisfaction with the outcome of your actions.

Eight of Pentacles

We usually work in order to obtain some result or other. But sometimes the work itself is the journey, the reward. We become one with what we are doing and strive to reach beyond our abilities toward something more.

Divinatory meaning: Working carefully.

Reversed: Doing sloppy work; not paying attention; brushing over important details.

Nine of Pentacles

This woman is justifiably pleased with her work. She has created a charming home filled with good things. Now that the hard work is done, she is in a position to enjoy herself.

Divinatory meaning: Accomplishment; justifiable pride in achievements.

Reversed: Doing things or creating things in order to meet emotional needs.

Ten of Pentacles

A family gathers in celebration. Generations represent the cycles of life and connections between people through time. The older generations cared for their homes and taught the younger. The younger, in their turn, will continue the traditions and care for the elders.

Divinatory meaning: Stable and abundant life.

Reversed: Having a stable life but finding it confining and a burden; staying in a place out of habit and security.

Ace of Swords

An athame's blade can, on a spiritual level, cut through superfluous or unnecessary energy. Once everything that is not needed – or is not the truth for that situation – is eliminated, then the truth of the matter can be seen.

Divinatory meaning: A new approach or solution to a problem.

Reversed: An idea or solution will not have the hoped for results. You don't have the all the facts.

Two of Swords

When the head and the heart are enemies, the person is paralyzed, unable to move. This state can be self-induced and exasperated. However, by tapping into the flow of the Universe, you can calm the warring parties, create peace, and thereby find the middle ground.

Divinatory meaning: Seeking balance between the heart and the mind.

Reversed: Refusing to deal with an issue.

Three of Swords

Sometimes communication is painfully clear. There is no pretending the truth is anything but what it is. It cuts. It hurts. And you don't have to pretend it doesn't.

Divinatory meaning: Sorrow caused by knowledge.

Reversed: Letting emotions make a situation worse than it is.

Four of Swords

There is always work to do. Things will always need attention. Problems forever seek solutions. Luckily, this woman has learned that sometimes the best ideas come when she takes a break. Relaxing her mind allows her to connect with the Divine, enjoy a moment of calm, and prepare for inspiration.

Divinatory meaning: Respite from troubles.

Reversed: Ignoring the need for rest or retreat.

Five of Swords

Our society encourages intense competition on many levels and in many areas of life. Even for those who "win" there can be conflicted feelings about the situation. Friendly competition is only a few steps removed from conflict. While winning can feel great, it can feel lots of other things, too.

Divinatory meaning: Mixed reactions in a competitive situation.

Reversed: A pyrrhic victory.

Six of Swords

It can be hard to extricate yourself from a dark or dangerous situation alone. Fortunately, help can usually be found. Seeking the truth for your highest good will reveal guidance for the way out. Hold tight to that truth and follow it until you're where you know you need to be.

Divinatory meaning: Guidance and help to leave a negative situation.

Reversed: Staying in a situation that could be escaped; disregarding help.

Seven of Swords

Trust can be breached in many ways. When we take what is not meant for us, we are behaving in a way that is counter to the truth. Because like attracts like, expressing untruthful energy attracts the same and creates more in the world. Whatever we create, we are responsible for.

Divinatory meaning: Someone taking something that doesn't belong to them.

Reversed: Having something taken from you.

Eight of Swords

This woman is in a complex situation. She has gathered all the facts, or so she thinks. She has devised complicated hypothesis and plans, yet they all seem to lead nowhere, or even worse, they make a bad situation even more impossible.

Divinatory meaning: Not knowing how to solve a problem or defuse a negative situation.

Reversed: Everything attempted makes things worse.

Nine of Swords

All sorts of thoughts and ideas dress themselves up as truth and come home to roost. They become very persistent and make it difficult to see other possibilities no matter how much better or close at hand they seem to be.

Divinatory meaning: The power of worry and regret.

Reversed: Severe nightmares and problems with insomnia.

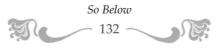

Ten of Swords

Our thoughts become reality. Dwelling too much on the past or hoping for things that cannot be prevents a healthy life from unfolding. This woman is ready to put an end to old thought patterns and unrealistic expectations. By doing so, she prepares her for new ways of thinking.

Divinatory meaning: Accepting and releasing unpleasant or unfortunate circumstances.

Reversed: Reliving heartache by refusing to let go.

Ace of Wands

All of the Aces represent gifts and opportunities. Although the strength of our will is always within us, at times we need a boost. Just when we need it the most, the Divine lights a fire and sends a little energy our way. When that happens, our actions are touched with magic.

Divinatory meaning: An opportunity to take action.

Reversed: An action does not yield the expected results. Rethink the plan.

Two of Wands

To accomplish anything, whether magical or otherwise, it is necessary to have a clear vision of the goal and to gather the necessary resources. This woman focuses her thoughts and her will, represented by the athame and the wand, on her desired outcome. She looks within to find her connection to the Universal Energy.

Divinatory meaning: Gathering energy while refining your vision.

Reversed: Changing your mind and losing focus.

Three of Wands

This woman has done all the necessary work, and her desire has been released to the Universe. Now, she waits, content within the flow of the Divine Energy and with perfect trust that her goal will manifest.

Divinatory meaning: Attracting a result.
Reversed: Wasting time and energy.

Four of Wands

This has planned this festival for quite a while. Many people working together toward a common goal is often cause for celebration, especially when the event goes off without a hitch, as this one appears to have.

Divinatory meaning: Celebrating the manifestation of a goal or other happy event.
Reversed: All work and no play.

Five of Wands

Working together can lead to fabulous results, as evidenced in the Four of Wands. However, getting to the result may be fraught with conflict and trouble, particularly when people feel very strongly about something. Egos and expectations get in the way of the easy flow of communally generated energy.

Divinatory meaning: Conflict.
Reversed: A highly charged situation gets dangerously out of hand.

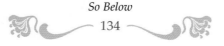

Six of Wands

This woman has focused her will and set her intention and has achieved great heights, quite literally. It is amazing what we can see when we overcome challenges and reach our highest potential. The recognition of others is always nice, but nothing really matches inner satisfaction.

Divinatory meaning: Achievement.

Reversed: Not valuing your accomplishments.

Seven of Wands

Even if we are not feeling perfectly confident inside, we can, like this woman, draw on the energy of the Universe help bolster us up a bit. The Universe has unlimited energy, so all we need to do is hold tight to our courage and ask for that boost to get us through.

Divinatory meaning: Having the strength to stand up for yourself and your ideas.

Reversed: Feeling defensive or overly protective.

Eight of Wands

The woman here has created her circle and called on the god and goddess and the quarters. She has raised the energy. She has the skill and experience to direct it. All of this is second nature to her. She is able to do it so quickly, so effortlessly, that she makes it look easy.

Divinatory meaning: Swift, controlled movement bringing a desired result.

Reversed: Chaotic events; a wrench in the machinery; sabotage.

Nine of Wands

Some challenges are harder than others. Nearing the end of her strength, this woman draws on the deepest reserves within her and prepares herself for what she knows will be the final encounter with this particular challenge. Weak, worn, and weary, she is not certain of the outcome, but she is prepared to give all that she can.

Divinatory meaning: Preparing for the final challenge.

Reversed: Giving up too soon.

Ten of Wands

It is easy to assume what success looks like. Our expectations shape so many of our actions. There are times when we will have a lot to carry and simply must do it. But sometimes we should ask the question: do I really need to carry this all right now? Just to make sure.

Divinatory meaning: Carrying a large burden or many burdens.

Reversed: Letting responsibilities slip through the cracks.

Court Cards

The Court Cards represent the people involved in whatever situation we are asking about. Many times the cards represent the querent, as they do usually have the most control over the events in their own lives. However, just as the Major Arcana cards often represent circumstances beyond our control, sometimes other people have authority or influence over our lives. If this is the case, they will show up in our readings. It is always useful to identify the roles, actions, and energies that people (including ourselves!) bring to a situation. We can then work with, channel, or perhaps defuse the energy or actions as necessary.

In *As Above*, we see the embodiment of the elements in their primal and archetypal forms. Here, we see how they are expressed in the roles we play in our everyday lives. To help illustrate the idea that we all take on various functions at different times in our lives, each court card in a suit features the same person. All of the Pages learn lessons relating to their suit. The Knights take some sort of action that expresses their suit. The Queens share their suit's energy directly with an individual. The Kings exercise their suit's power within a group.

To further illustrate how anyone can take on any of these characteristics, the As Below court cards use male figures for the Cups and Pentacles, which are traditionally considered feminine suits, and female figures for Swords and Wands, which are generally depicted as masculine.

The **Page of Cups** explores his intuition and dreams.
Reversed: Being overly sensitive.

The **Knight of Cups** delves into his imagination to visualize his heart's desire.
Reversed: Escapes into a fantasy world.

The **Queen of Cups** provides comfort and solace for an aching heart.
Reversed: Encourages drama and feeds off emotional turmoil.

The **King of Cups** encourages others to express themselves and share their hearts.
Reversed: Is disconnected from his emotions and others.

The **Page of Pentacles** studies the rhythms of nature and learns the secrets of the physical realm.
Reversed: Greedy and self-serving.

The **Knight of Pentacles** works with the energy of the land to manifest his will.
Reversed: Focuses only on outcomes and monetary gain.

The **Queen of Pentacles** teaches others how to relate to nature and the physical world in a personal way.
Reversed: Cares more about appearances than substance.

The **King of Pentacles** shares the delights and wonders of the physical generously with others.
Reversed: Tries to buy people's affections or obedience by controlling resources.

The **Page of Swords** experiments with ideas, thought systems, and philosophies.
Reversed: Suspicious, prone to gossip, and sometimes untruthful.

The **Knight of Swords** wields the power of her mind and knowledge of language to achieve her goals.
Reversed: Manipulative and often judgmental.

The **Queen of Swords** uses her skills to help someone focus her actions by eliminating the unnecessary and highlighting the essential.
Reversed: Harsh, sarcastic, and sometimes cruel.

The **King of Swords** skillfully plans so that the group achieves greatness and individuals can shine.
Reversed: Motivates groups to achieve personal agendas, regardless of the cost to others.

The **Page of Wands** discovers both the dangers and the power of her will.
Reversed: Reckless and prone to taking risks.

The **Knight of Wands** focuses her will and gathers her power.
Reversed: Obsessive.

The **Queen of Wands** encourages expression of passion within a safe environment.
Reversed: Surrounds self with others in order to be the center of attention.

The **King of Wands** helps others to live their passion and realize their potential.
Reversed: Uses charisma to control others and feed her ego.

READING THE CARDS

Reading with Tarot cards

Doing a reading with tarot cards is an act of divination, a way of accessing Divine wisdom. Therefore, more than anything else, divination is about learning to listen. When we come to the cards with a question, we are asking the Divine to speak to us through the images on the cards. Using the cards, we can connect with the Divine and tune into the Universal flow. By reading the cards, we are able to see trends and possibilities that allow us to identify probable forecasts about the future. We can use that clear picture to know what energies are present and which are moving toward us. We use our knowledge of and experience with energy to determine how it will respond. In short, we can see the big picture and determine how best to act within it.

Before you begin, decide what question you want to ask and which spread you will use to answer it. Looking at the spreads and reading through the positions can help you clarify your question.
After you've settled on your question, select a spread that will help the cards and Divine express the answer in the clearest possible way.

As you prepare for your reading, ground yourself and then shuffle the cards. Lay them out, face up, as described in the spread. Take a few deep breaths, ask the Goddess and God to guide you, and begin to interpret the spread.
As you may imagine, there are so many other techniques and methods that can be used in reading the cards. As you work with your cards, you will develop your own. Also, there are plenty of books with ideas to try.

Suggested Reading List
Tarot Wisdom by Rachel Pollack
21 Ways to Read a Tarot Card by Mary K. Greer
Tarot for Beginners by Barbara Moore
Tarot 101 by Kim Huggens

Suggestion for selecting your question.

1. *Don't ask if you really don't want to know the answer. Before doing the reading, think about the worse answer you can imagine and how you would feel if that were was the answer. The good thing about the future is that pagans know it isn't written in stone and that we have free will and the ability to, in large part, create our own reality. So whatever you see in the cards, you can probably change or alter. But still, sometimes people aren't ready for that.*

2. *Ask questions that empower you and encourage you to take positive action for the greatest good.*

3. *If your readings aren't making sense and don't seem to answer your question, maybe you are asking the wrong question. Look at the reading and see if the Divine isn't trying to give you a message about something different.*

Spreads

Spreads are the way we lay out the cards selected for a reading. They help frame the answer both by their positional meanings and by their visual impact. The of the spread allows certain cards to interact with each other, providing nuances of meanings. When interpreting the cards always pay attention to how their energy interacts with the energy of nearby cards as well as what the position means.

The first few spreads are designed to work with one deck, although feel free to experiment mixing both decks, *As Above* and So Below. In general, *As Above* works better in smaller spreads and So Below is well suited for larger spreads. The following section, Double Deck Techniques, provides spreads and techniques that incorporate both decks.

Past Present Future Spread

A simple three-card spread provides a general overview of a situation. Three cards can provide plenty of information. Most importantly, it shows the strongest energies at play in the situation. Pay attention to how they either blend together, showing a smooth transition of events, or how they might be at odds, indicating possible conflict.

1. Past
2. Present
3. Future

Two Choices Spread

This is another useful three-card spread if you are facing two choices about a situation. When considering the options, imagine how the energies of first Choice A and then Choice B will interact with the dilemma or situation.

1. The dilemma or situation
2. Choice A
3. Choice B

Pentagram Advice Spread

This five-card spread was designed to provide advice from five different aspects of your Higher Self.

1. What your body wants you to know about the situation.
2. What your intellect wants you to know about the situation.
3. What your emotions want you to know about the situation.
4. What your will wants you to know about the situation.
5. What your spirit wants you to know about the situation.

The New Moon Spread

This spread illuminates issues, situations, or energies present in the current lunar cycle, specifically something that will begin, grow, and manifest during this month. It is meant to be performed on the dark (or new) moon. Each card represents a week in the lunar cycle.

1. New moon: what is beginning to unfold during this cycle.
2. Waxing moon: how it will progress.
3. Full moon: how it will manifest.
4. Waning moon: what to reflect on.
5. Next new moon: the outcome and seed for the cycle.

Celtic Cross Spread

The Celtic Cross Spread is a very traditional and well-known spread. It provides a variety of information about any situation. In this spread, it is interesting to compare the fifth, sixth, and tenth cards, as they all have to do with the future and outcomes.

1. You: this card represents you.
2. Crossing: the card indicates the conflict.
3. Foundation: this card illustrates the basis or foundation of the situation.
4. Past: this card shows influences from the past that are affecting the present situation.
5. Immediate Future: this card illustrates what is likely to happen next.

6. Crown: this card represents the outcome you desire most in this situation.

7. Yourself: this is your self-image; how you see yourself in the present situation.

8. Environment: this card represents the influences of those around you; it can show how others see you in this situation.

9. Hopes and Fears: this card indicates either what you hope for or fear the most in this situation.

10. Outcome: what is likely to happen if nothing changes.

The Big Picture Spread

This is a large spread that provides plenty of detail about a situation, including how it came to be, what is affecting it now, the energies that will shape it in the near future, and the probable outcome. There are three optional cards that can be added at the end. If you are not content with the probable outcome, these three cards will give advice on how to change it. The spread lends itself to using both decks. Draw cards 1, 6, 9, and 11 from *As Above* and the rest from *So Below*. This will provide an even larger view of the energies affecting the situation.

Cards 1, 2, and 3: The energies currently affecting the situation.

Cards 4, 5, and 6: How the past has shaped this situation.

Cards 7, 8, and 9: What energy will influence the resolution.

Cards 10, 11, and 12: The probable outcome.

Optional cards 13, 14, and 15: Energy that you can use or actions you can take to alter the outcome, if desired.

Double Deck Techniques

The two decks that together make The *Book of Shadows Tarot*, *As Above* and *So Below*, were designed to reflect the pagan experience. *As Above* holds our beliefs and illustrates universal energies. *So Below* expresses how those beliefs manifest in this world and details our personal energy or how we work with universal energy. This unique two-deck system allows for powerful readings.

Reading with two decks is not entirely new. Many tarot readers have experimented with the idea. The comparative method gained in popularity in the past decade. This is a method where the reader selects the same card from two or more decks and compares them in order to form a deeper meaning or receive a fuller message. Another way two decks have been used in the same reading is if the question is about a relationship or comparing two choices, the reader may use one deck to represent one person or idea and a different deck for the other. The uniquely designed *Book of Shadows Tarot* decks can of course be used in those ways. Below, you will find other ways that these two decks work together.

The traditional structure of the *So Below* Tarot provides a foundation for most of the double deck reading techniques. The unique structure of *As Above* Tarot gives more focus and precision to the readings. Most of the double deck readings require dividing *As Above* into smaller decks while *So Below* is generally used in its entirety. When interpreting the cards in these spreads, you will rely less on the divinatory meanings for the cards from *As Above*. Instead you will focus on the spirit of the meaning and energy described.

As Above, So Below Technique
The easiest way to combine the two decks is to lay out your reading as usual (or consider just drawing one card as the answer to your question), using either deck. Then go through the other deck and select the same cards, laying them next to the each other in the

spread and reading the two cards as a pair. Pay particular attention to the energy available, indicated by the *As Above* card, in relation to what the querent is doing with that energy, indicated by the *So Below* card.

The cards can always be used in this manner. As the reading progresses, if there are a preponderance of reversed cards and the querent wished to unblock the energy, identify the beginning of the block in the spread, usually the first *So Below* card before the series of reversed cards. This card is coupled with energy that should be flowing but is not. This is likely because the querent is not utilizing the energy in the best way. Shuffle the remaining *So Below* cards, ask for guidance on how the querent can best use that energy to restore the natural flow, and draw a card. Place that card on top of the blocking card. Turn the following cards right-side up and reinterpret the spread to discover what will happen if the querent behaves differently.

The Energetic Add-On
Determine your question, select your spread, and lay out a reading in the usual manner using the *So Below* Tarot. Before proceeding to the interpretation, divide your *As Above* Tarot into two piles: the Major cards and the Minor cards. Shuffle and randomly draw one Major card and place it at the very top of your reading. This card provides the main focal point of reading and all other cards should be read in relation to it. Then draw three cards at random from the Minors. Place one at the bottom of your reading and one on either side. These cards represent energy or resources that are not currently engaged in the situation but are available to you and can be used to change an undesirable outcome or facilitate a positive outcome.

Reality vs. Perception Reading
This deceptively simple reading can pack a lot of power if the querent is prepared to be honest with themselves.

There are four positions in this spread but you will deal out two cards for each position, one from each deck. The card from *As Above* goes above the card from *So Below*. The cards are laid out in a line.

The heart of the question
The challenge
Advice
Outcome

The top row, *As Above*, shows what is happening on a spiritual level. The bottom row shows how the spiritual influences are manifesting in the querent's life. If there is a disconnect between the top and the bottom card, this shows an area where the querent needs to examine their opinion and perhaps reconsider their actions.

The Sphere of Influence
This spread is done after a regular reading using *So Below* if the outcome is not to the querent's liking. Gather up the cards from the reading except for the one that represents the undesired outcome. Place that card in the center of the reading space. Have the querent go through the deck and pick on that represents the ideal outcome and place that card on top of the first card.

Divide your *As Above* deck into five sections: the Majors, Air, Fire, Water, Earth, and Court cards.

Pull one card from each and place around two original cards. The Major card shows the largest challenge that separates the predicted outcome from the desired outcome. The Air, Fire, Water, and Earth cards show the energy present that can possibly be used or channeled. The Court Card gives an idea of how easily the outcome can be changed. The Element card represents the easiest situation to change, while the Crone is the other end of the spectrum, showing a situation that is nearly completed and therefore difficult to change.